Chris

Fashion Window Shopping

©2013 CHOIS PUBLISHING INC.

ISBN 978-1-61175-044-7 / 1-61175-044-X

CHOIS PUBLISHING INC.
P.O.Box 4389, Road Town, Tortola, British Virgin Islands
China Office
Unit 1201, Anji Plaza, 760 S. Xizang Rd., Shanghai 200011, China
Email: info@choisgallery.com
Phone: +86 21 6346 0711/10

Publisher
David Choi

Editorial & Art Department
Editorial Director: Lynn Lin
Executive Editor: Cynthia Hsu
cynthia@choisgallery.com
Art Director: Fanghong Wang
Proofreading Editor: Susie Gordon
Designer: Wei Dai

Marketing & Sales Department
Advertising Inquiries: Claudia Chen
claudia.chen@choisgallery.com

Sales Executive (Overseas): Shannon Ye
dist@choisgallery.com

Subscriptions: Pete Yu
pete@choisgallery.com

Marketing Manager (China): Nomi Wu
wuguo@choisgallery.com

Distributor
Chois Publishing Inc. Taiwan office
No. 11, Section 3, Héping East Rd, Daan District, Taipei City 10675, Taiwan
Phone: 02-23042764

Kili China
Unit 1201, Anji Plaza, 760 S. Xizang Rd., Shanghai 200011, China
Phone: +86 21 6346 0711/10
info@choisgallery.com

Share Your Genius With The Global Peers.
Please visit **www.choisgallery.com** or contact Cynthia Hsu:
cynthia@choisgallery.com to contribute your fantastic work.

Printed and Bound in China

Sharing the Wisdom of Global Innovation

In a scientific sense, the art world contains no initiators or precursors. However, unlike science, the works of our predecessors do not constitute an acquired truth from which anyone who follows after can profit. That is why today, even if you try your best to write, it is not possible to match great writers like Homer.

Most of us are just passengers in the creative field, but we thirst for our peers' experiences in creating. In the meantime, we like to share our accomplishments with them. It is hard to believe that in this era of free information, what we know is still limited and incomplete. The Internet, which most people believe to be a panacea, brings too much confusion and too many choices, and this truth is unfortunately neglected.

In the past two years, Chois Publishing Inc. has published a series of magazines and books about the creative industry, such as Gallery (the world's best graphics) bimonthly and Choi's Package quarterly. We prefer print media - the traditional way to spread new ideas — because we believe that it holds inherent value and is a better way to showcase the work in detail. More importantly, it displays the integrity and ability required in this "hand-made" industry.

To quote George Bernard Shaw: "If you have an apple and I have an apple and we exchange apples, then you and I will still each have one apple. But if you have an idea and I have an idea and we exchange these ideas, then each of us will have two ideas. "

Through this "SHARING PLAN" we hope to facilitate the exchange of ideas. We are not merely focusing on the graphics, but dealing with the whole creative industry, including architecture, interiors, fashion, and product design. We warmly welcome you to join us.

With thanks.
The Editor

CONTENTS

Fantasy

Modern

 # Nature 180

 # Pop 218

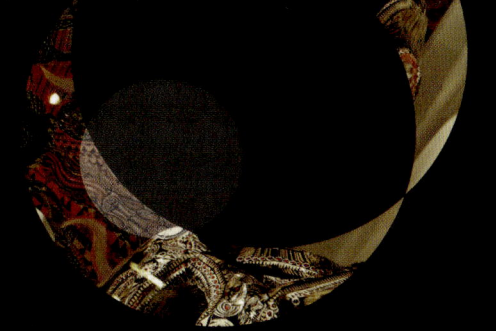

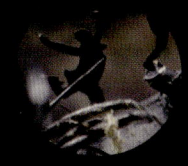

Fantasy

Topshop Christmas 2010

D1 Design & Creative worked in conjunction with Topshop to create their white winter Christmas window scheme. The flagship at Oxford Street proved the highlight with a giant working snow globe feature, within which were several styled mannequins. D1 also designed, produced and installed mirror distressed plinths and cascading crystal backdrops for the rollout across Topshop flagship stores throughout UK and New York.

Client_ **TOPSHOP** | Design_ **D1 DESIGN & CREATIVE** | Photography_ **MELVYN VINCENT** | Year of completion_ **2010** | Country_ **UK**

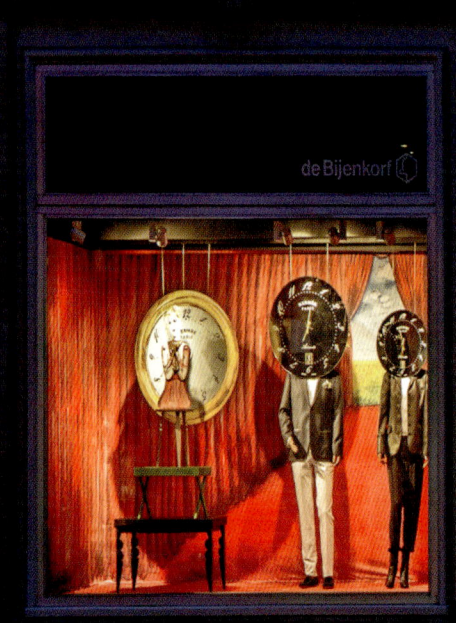

Hermès Windows At Bijenkorf Amsterdam

Hermès gave carte blanche to Kiki to create five exceptional windows at the Bijenkorf Amsterdam. Kiki designed all five windows within the concept "the gift of time", which is the 2012 theme of Hermès windows. "Time is even more precious now than before. It's the biggest jewel you can have. Why not juggle with time, and show the different aspects of it? It's all about your perception of time. In those five windows I'm showing five different ways of how you could look at time, in a very playful way, inspired by the philosophy and history of Hermès. It really shows the joy of a child playing with a lot of fantasy, like Alice in Wonderland." >>

The corner window shows a playground of time. A knife pitcher throws clock hands at a huge clock. At the same time, three moons show the time: London- Paris- New York. Everyone is doing different tricks! >>

Window 1 displays the importance of balancing your time. A dandy walking on stilts is balancing the time with a carriage wheel with clock on his right foot , and a chair with cuckoo clock in his left hand. >>

Window 2 demonstrates the juggle with time. A dandy is juggling with a high head and a scarf, sometimes showing the time, sometimes not, while a rabbit is moving away from the scenery with a clock in its hand.
>>

Window 3 implies that humans hold the centre of time.
A woman stands in the middle of a clock, pointing the
time with an umbrella and twirl stick in her arms. She
has two assistants dressed in Hermès clothing, wearing
a mirrored clock instead of human faces. >>

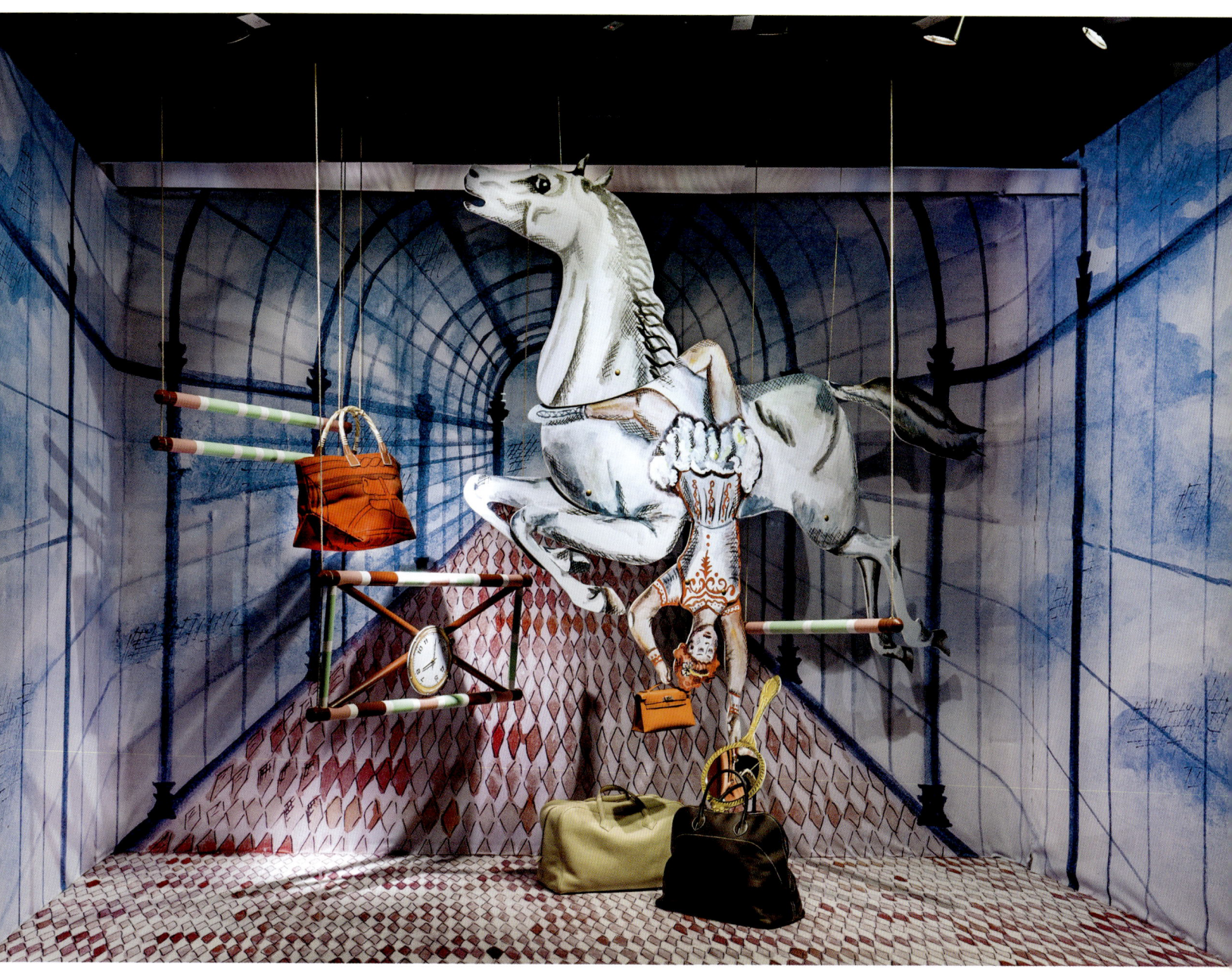

Window 4 presents mirrors and playing with time.
An acrobat girl is hanging from the back of a horse,
which is jumping over horizontal bars. She holds
a mirror, in which time that works backwards is
reflected.

Client_ **HERMÈS** | Design_ **KIKI VAN EIJK** | Photography_ **FRANK TIELEMANS** | Year of completion_ **2012** | Country_ **THE NETHERLANDS**

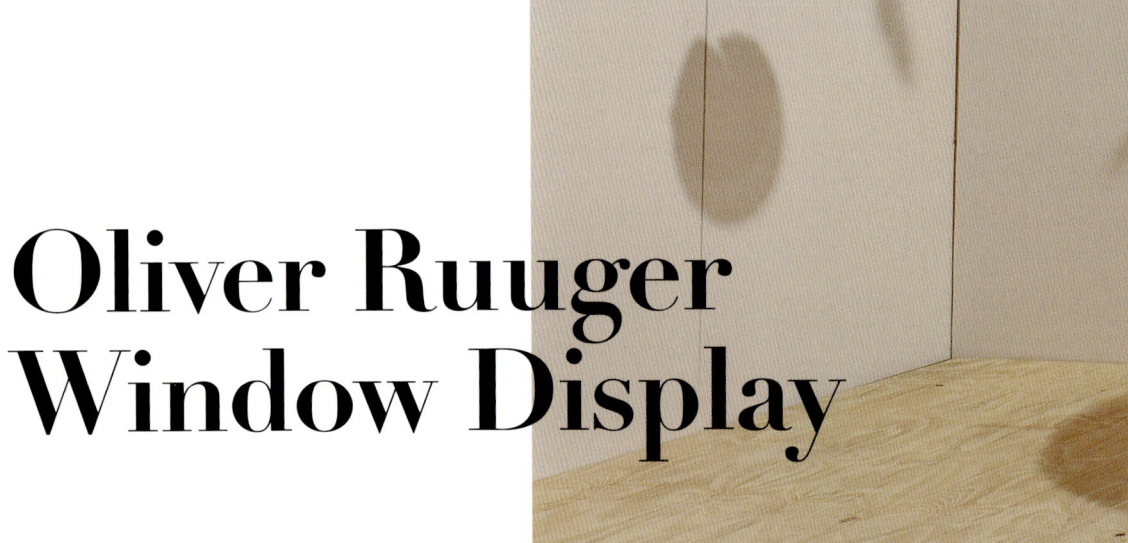

Oliver Ruuger
Window Display

CHAPTER VIII

OLIVER
RUUGER

Accessories Designer
oliverruuger.com

BRIGHT
YOUNG
THINGS

#SelfridgesBYT

www.selfridges.co

Oliver Ruuger has created a window installation of floating still life, consisting of fifteen separately suspended pieces. The objects are set in a manner to suggest an idea of wind and movement, from right to left. A studded briefcase opens and unveils a book, spilling its pages into the wind. The sheets roll and turn into abstract storm birds, which are carrying huge eggs. A few eggs have been dropped and broken into several pieces to reveal stunning umbrellas.

Oliver Ruuger was inspired by Philippe Halsman's photograph of Salvador Dali, named Aotmicus. It involves three cats being tossed by three assistants, a bucket of water being thrown, and Dali leaping in front of a canvas with a paintbrush in his hand. It is all about surreal movement within a static display; a portrait. Oliver Ruuger wanted to approach the window display in a similar manner, conveying movement in something which one expects to be static and adding a surreal storyline for the viewer to discover.

Design_ **OLIVER RUUGER** Photography_ **OLIVER RUUGER** Country_ **UK**

Barneys Window Display

Client_ **BARNEYS**   Design_ **DENNIS MCNETT**   Photography_ **BRYCE WARD**   Year of completion_ **2011**   Country_ **USA**

Black And Gold Wonderland

*I*n October 2010, Diesel approached me to collaborate with WONDERLAND MAGAZINE to design a Christmas scheme for their London flagship store on New Bond Street. As well as producing the windows, the brief was to extend the design through into as much of the store as possible, so that visitors to the store could feel they were immersed in the experience. Referencing Diesel Black and Gold, we created a dark wonderland made up of painted trees, foliage and small paper "traveler" making their way to a hand-made golden temple inside the forest.

Client_ **DIESEL**   Design_ **KYLE BEAN**   Photography_ **LEX KEMBERY**   Year of completion_ **2010**   Country_ **UK**

High Fliers

*F*ounded in 2008, London-based architecture practice Liddicoat & Goldhill focuses on making. They are the hands-on protagonist of their work. Their interest lies in the haptic, the imagined and the poetry of practical things. They work with humble materials in practical environments to create the unexpected.
RIBA London hit the shops on Regent Street in April 2012 with a new window installation project produced around the theme of "PLAY" in collaboration with the Regent Street Association and media partner ELLE Decoration.

Liddicoat & Goldhill were one of nine architects to be selected to produce a window installation along Regent Street, chosen by shirt retailer T.M.Lewin, They were challenged to create a spatial installation to reflect their retail partners' brand.
Entitled "High Fliers", Liddicoat & Goldhill's scheme mixed the theme of "Play" with T.M.Lewint brand concept of "Performance". The outdoor exhibition ran from 16th April to 6th May and saw London's skyline play host to a cluster of serene origami balloons. Using the shirt-maker's crisp folding and cutting techniques, fabrics in multifarious patterns and hues were reshaped into three-dimensional high-flying lanterns.

Client_ **T.M.LEWIN & RIBA** | Design_ **LIDDICOAT & GOLDHILL** | Photography_ **TOM GILDON** | Year of completion_ **2012** | Country_ **UK**

Hermès Windows
From Amsterdam To Milano

After the big success of the windows designed for Hermès at the Bijenkorf Amsterdam, Kiki was asked by Hermès Italy to adapt those five exceptional windows into an installation of eight windows for their Milano store during the Salone del Mobile. In the eight windows, Kiki showed different ways of how one could look at time, in a very playful way, inspired by the philosophy and history of Hermès.

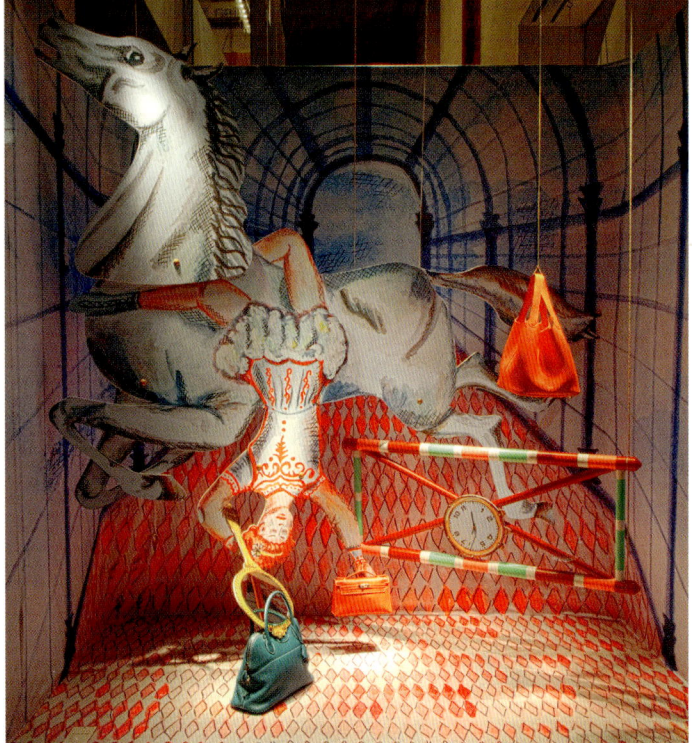

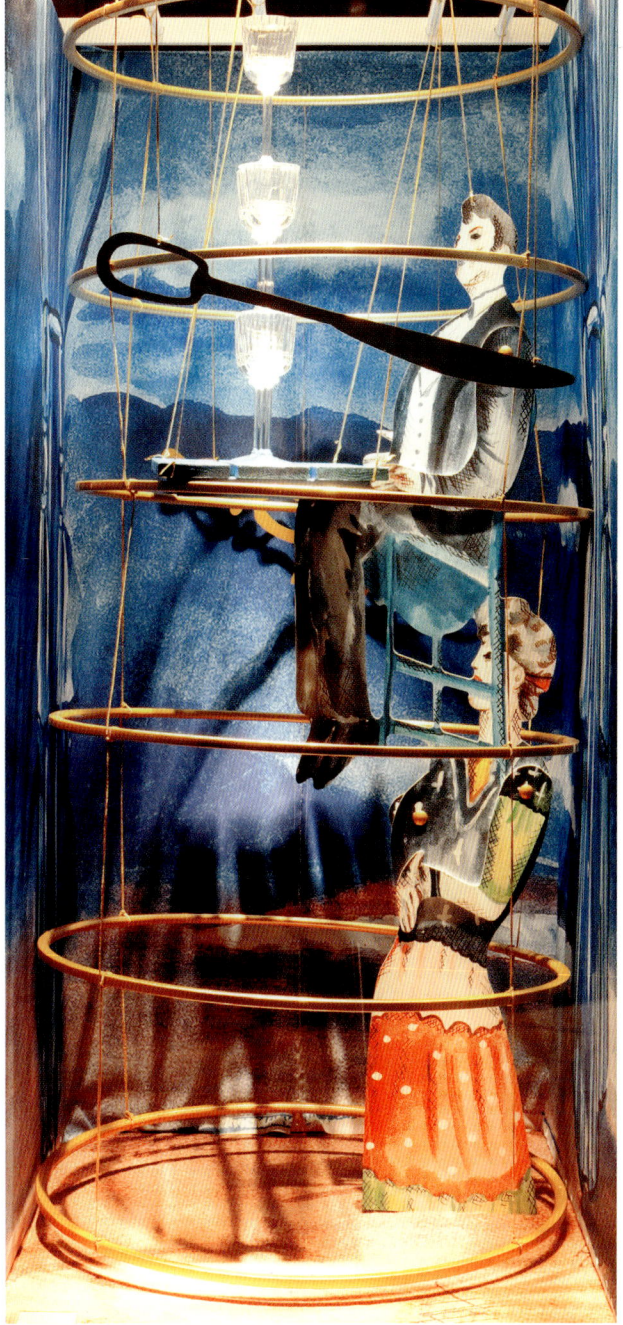

Galeria Kaufhof
Summer Campaign 2012

*T*he Galeria Kaufhof GmbH is one of Europe's leading companies in running department stores. After our first successful collaboration in 2009, we had the chance to develop the 2012 summer campaign. Yet again, we worked in close cooperation with Kaufhof's team of designers. We created a total of three jungle motifs, which served as a stage for mannequins and products in the shop windows of all 109 stores across Germany.

The distinctive feature of these pictures, and what makes them so special, is that all the landscapes depicted consist of products that can be bought inside the shops. Even before a test assembling took place and preliminary combinations of products, mannequins and images were put together, we could already check three-dimensional effects using short clips created within the 3D software.

Client_ **GALERIA KAUFHOF**   Design_ **VIAFRAME**   Photography_ **VIAFRAME**   Year of completion_ **2012**   Country_ **GERMANY**

Swan Lake

Christmas 2011 window display for one of London's leading advertising agencies. Inspired by Swan Lake, we created a three-metre-tall swan for the agency's foyer, as well as ballet shoes, baubles and a curtain of smaller swans for the nine-floor staircase.

Client_ **AMV BBDO**   Design_ **THE MAKERIE STUDIO**   Photography_ **THE MAKERIE STUDIO**   Year of completion_ **2011**   Country_ **UK**

Charles Vögele
Autumn Campaign 2012

*W*e developed a total of five ad-campaign motives for the autumn advertising campaign of the Swiss fashion store Charles Vögele.
Autumn leaves, rain and clouds shape animals which are placed into autumn landscapes.
The motives we created were used in different formats at the point of sale of over 850 stores. They are located in Switzerland, Germany, Austria, Belgium, Netherlands, Slovenia, Hungary as well as the Czech Republic and Poland.

Client_ **CHARLES VÖGELE**   Design_ **VIAFRAME**   Photography_ **VIAFRAME**   Year of completion_ **2012**   Country_ **GERMANY**

Hermès Window Display

*W*indow display illustrations for French high fashion house Hermès, showcased in seven of their stores on the east coast of US. The illustrated wooden panels were flexible backdrops to showcase the Hermès summer collection.

Charles Vögele
Spring Campaign
2011

*F*or the Charles Vögele spring campaign, six
themes based on blossoms were created. The look,
visual conception as well as the colours were selected in
close collaboration with the customer.

Client_ **CHARLES VÖGELE**   Design_ **VIAFRAME**   Photography_ **VIAFRAME**   Year of completion_ **2011**   Country_ **GERMANY**

KYLE BEAN

blink

'Matter cannot be created or destroyed, only transformed.'

The law of conservation of mass

www.kylebean.co.uk
www.blinkart.co.uk

Transformation

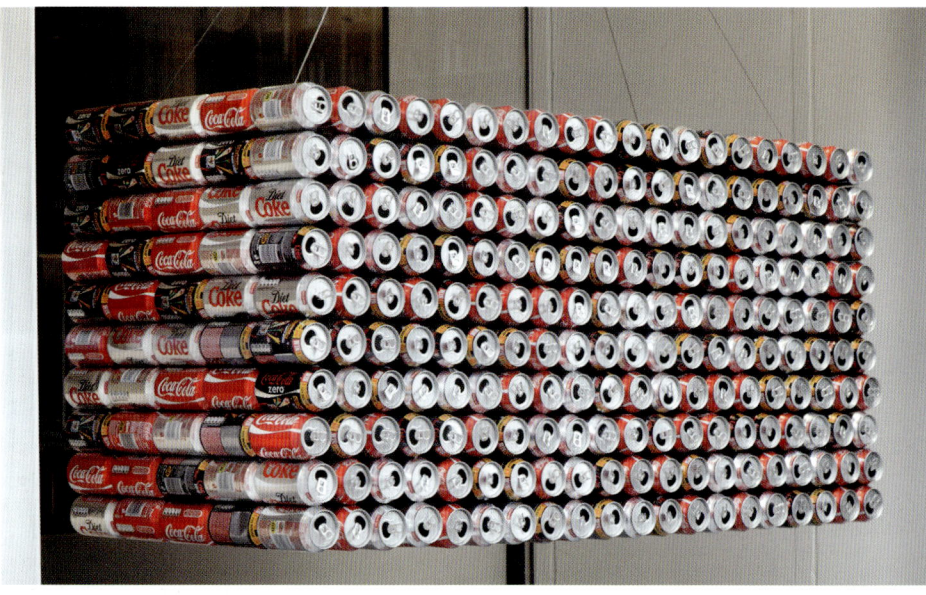

*I*nspired by the law of conservation of mass, "Matter cannot be created or destroyed, only transformed", my concept was that in each window I would show one object, but each object would be transformed in some way, showing it therefore in two different states. Each object would then be suspended on one side of a giant set of hanging scales, showing that they are essentially the same, just transformed. One window included a wedding cake, with all of its ingredients hung like a mobile on the other side, a fairytale castle constructed by hand from pages from old fairytale books, and 1000 aluminium cans compacted down into a small cube, alongside another 1000 cans, arranged like a grid into another giant cube. The largest window showcased two real motorbikes hung from the scales, one in its normal state and the other disassembled into all of its component parts.

KYLE BEAN

'Matter cannot be created or destroyed, only transformed.'

The law of conservation of mass

www.kylebean.co.uk
www.blinkart.co.uk

Client_ **SELFRIDGES**   Design_ **KYLE BEAN**   Photography_ **ANDREW MEREDITH MIKE DODD**   Year of completion_ **2010**   Country_ **UK**

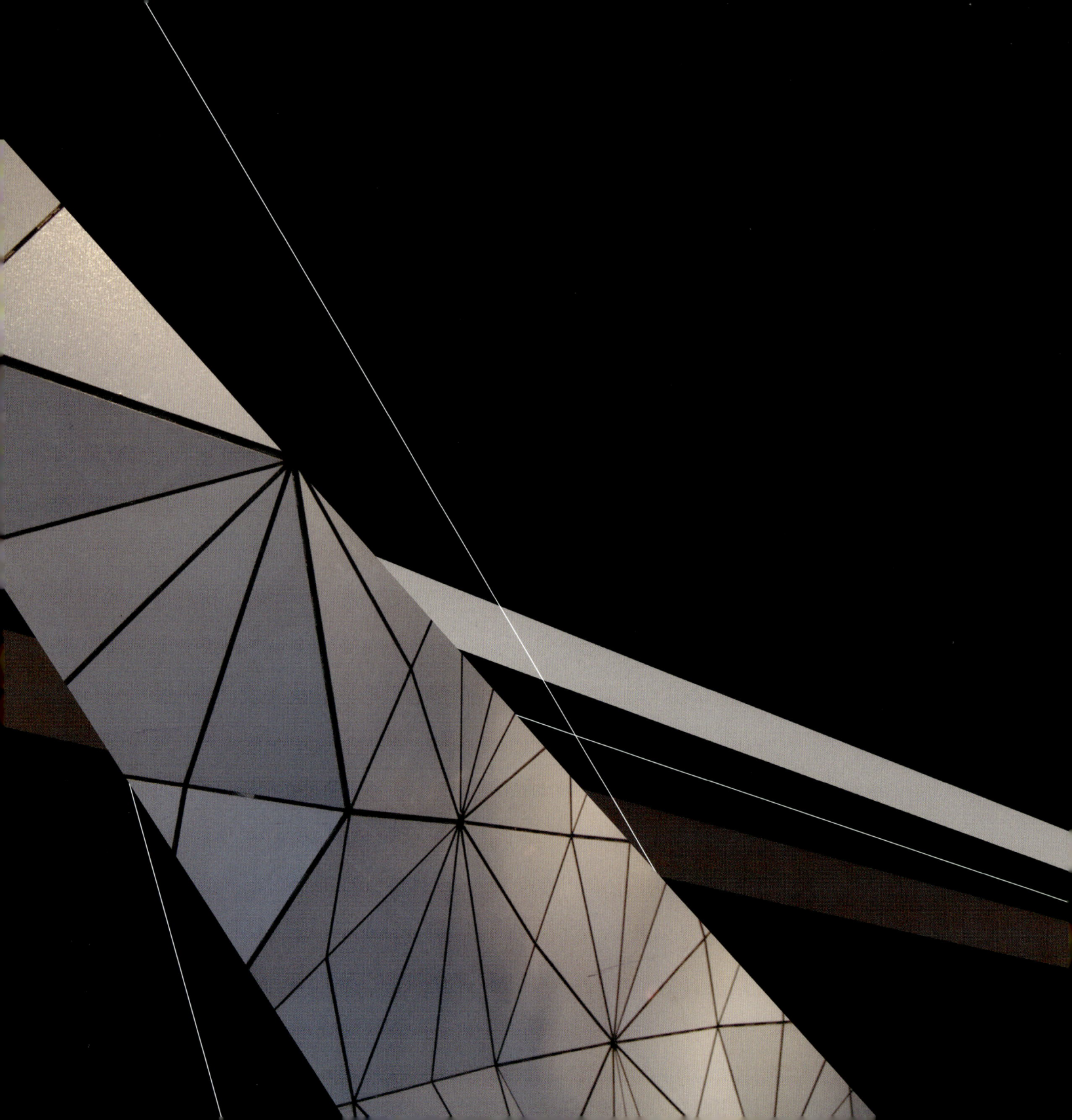

Aberrant Architecture
× MF Art

A berrant architecture resurrects the social past times of the historic Shanghai Race club by staging an interactive horse race in the windows of MF Art+. The model race track transforms customers into horse jockeys. Miniature horses mounted on race-cars are controlled by shoppers and speed around a track in the window of the MF Art+ store.
The installation invites everyone to compete.

RIBA PLAY YOUR STYLE @ XINTIANDI, SHANGHAI 2012

JNBY + Croquis
Window Display

*M*o.ron × Croquis
A synthetic landscape of cardboard tubes sweeps across the shop window and store interior, creating a dramatic backdrop for product display. Simple material components are combined to create complex forms, mirroring the Croquis brand ethos.

Mo.ron × JNBY
Dense clusters of interlinking triangular panels engulf the store entrance and punch through the window façade. The careful cutting and stitching of repeated elements creates an intricate sculpture and responds to the JNBY clothing.

Client_ **JNBY + CROQUIS**   Design_ **MOXON**   Photography_ **JAN SIEFKE**   Year of completion_ **2012**   Country_ **UK**

CHAPTER X

ALICE LEE

Womenswear Desig
aliceelee.co.uk

BRIGHT YOUNG THINGS

#Selfridges-BYT
www.selfridges.

Alice Lee Window Display

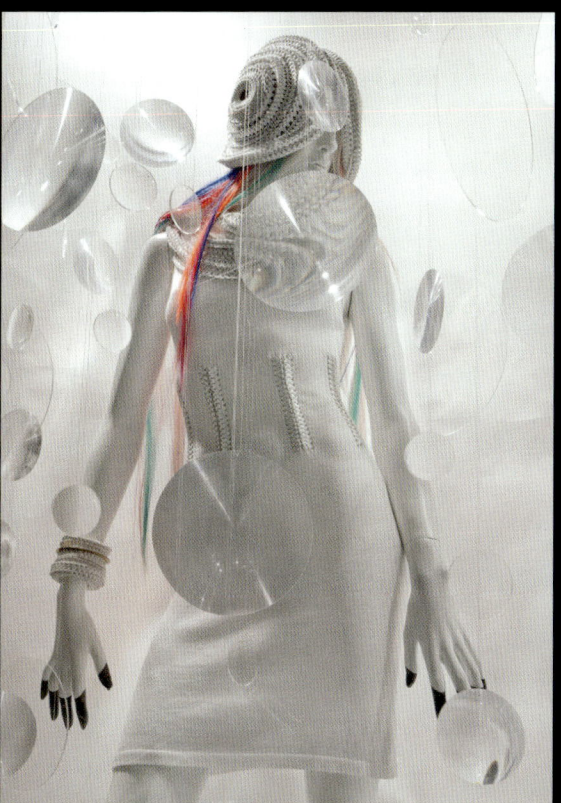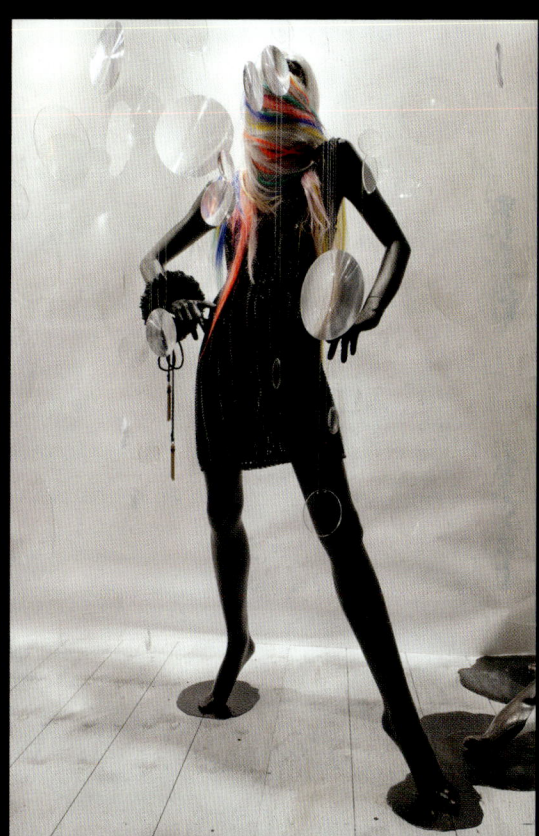

Aluminium Plates

ISABEL MARANT

ALUMINIUM BEIRUT

A *luminum plate series by Arnold Goron for Isabel Marant. Pine wood structure and aluminum snail plates stapled together. Snail plates have a particular aesthetic compared to other aluminum plates, and it's so French.*

ALUMINIUM TOKYO

Client_ **ISABEL MARANT**   Design_ **ARNOLD GORON**   Photography_ **ARNOLD GORON**   Year of completion_ **2012**   Country_ **FRANCE**

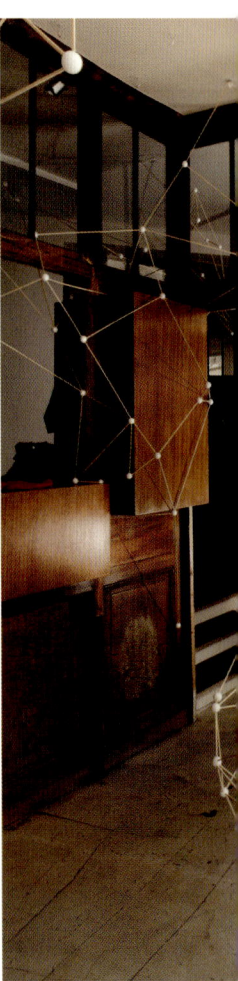

Molecular Structures

*S*tructures made of samba wood connected with
styrofoam balls and electric motors.

Client_ **ISABEL MARANT**   Design_ **ARNOLD GORON**   Photography_ **ARNOLD GORON**   Year of completion_ **2011**   Country_ **FRANCE**

Porcelain Bird

*S*tructure made of 350 translucent porcelain biscuit
feathers (*KERAFOL green tape*), wingspan 3m.
All feathers hang together by nylon string .

Client_ **ISABEL MARANT**　　　Design_ **ARNOLD GORON**　　　Photography_ **ARNOLD GORON**　　　Year of completion_ **2009**　　　Country_ **FRANCE**

Spring Mobiles

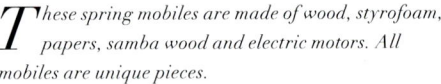
These spring mobiles are made of wood, styrofoam, papers, samba wood and electric motors. All mobiles are unique pieces.
As there is not enough wind in the shop, I used a motor to make the mobiles spin into the window.

Client_ **ISABEL MARANT**   Design_ **ARNOLD GORON**   Photography_ **ARNOLD GORON, IT**   Year of completion_ **2012**   Country_ **FRANCE**

Chairman Ting ×
Adidas Shanghai

*C*hairman Ting was invited to collaborate with adidas Shanghai to help create a fun winter themed window display for the launch of the adidas winter collection while promoting Chairman Ting's art exhibition. Each character design in the store is custom made for adidas by Chairman Ting.

After our success with adidas Originals × Forces of Nice art show collaboration in Hong Kong in September 2010, adidas asked if we could do more work for them in Shanghai. We were given the store layout and the winter collection they wanted to feature this season. We came back to them a week later after our briefing with rough sketches for their approval and within 48 hours we were already into full production.

The illustrations took Carson a week of endless nights to complete while Denise took care of all the business meetings in Hong Kong. A few days before the launch, adidas flew Denise and Sophia Tong of OslerZoo Photography to Shanghai from HK to help set up and make sure everything was looking exactly how we envisioned it.

Needless to say, the fine marketing folks at adidas were extremely happy with how it all turned out. The custom adidas art and our Chairman Ting art collection was open for public viewing at the adidas IFC store in Shanghai China until December 31, 2010.

Client_ **ADIDAS**   Design_ **CHAIRMAN TING**   Design team_ **CARSON TING DENISE CHEUNG**   Photography_ **OSLERZOO PHOTOGRAPHY**   Year of completion_ **2010**   Country_ **CANADA**

LOREAK MENDÌAN

Además

A window display featuring three Además T-shirts from the spring/summer collection, supported by the arm of a tripod, placed between three raised-bed canopies, which in turn support a pair of Vans.

Client_ **LOREAK MENDIAN**   Design_ **JA! STUDIO**   Photography_ **FLORO AZQUETA**   Country_ **SPAIN**

Emilita

A *window display featuring three Emilita T-shirts and various items from the spring/summer collection supported by two stepladders, one on top of the other.*

LOREAK MENDIAN

Client_ **LOREAK MENDIAN**   Design_ **JA! STUDIO**   Photography_ **FLORO AZQUETA**   Country_ **SPAIN**

Eusko Label

A conceptual window display, showing the company's denim jeans from the spring/summer 2010 collection.

Client_ **LOREAK MENDIAN**   Design_ **JA! STUDIO**   Photography_ **FLORO AZQUETA**   Country_ **SPAIN**

Loreak Mendia
Colección Primavera
Verano 2011

High Spirits

A window display featuring a background of acoustic
panels made from recycled foam showcasing items
from the 2011 spring/summer collection.

| Client_ **LOREAK MENDIAN** | Design_ **JA! STUDIO** | Photography_ **FLORO AZQUETA** | Country_ **SPAIN** |

Krampen

*A window display featuring one of the prints and
shoes from the autumn/winter 2010/2011 collection
on top of three different chairs.*

Client_ **LOREAK MENDIAN**   Design_ **JA! STUDIO**   Photography_ **FLORO AZQUETA**   Country_ **SPAIN**

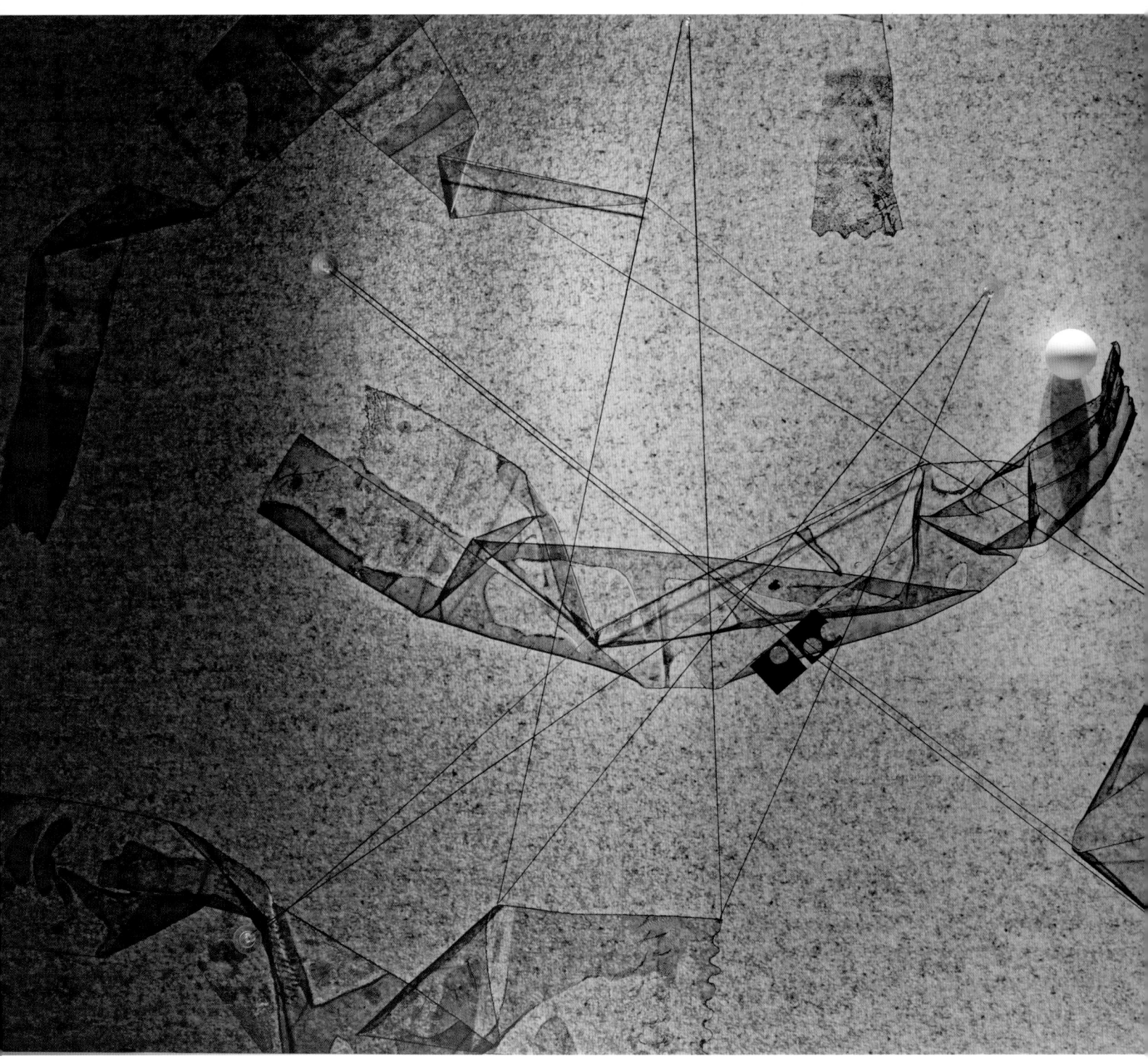

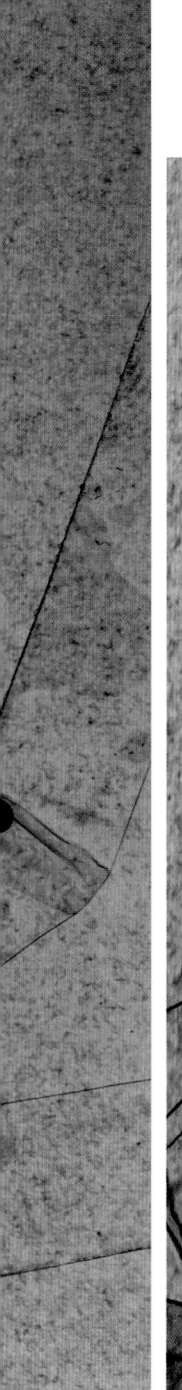

Pelotari

A conceptual Christmas window display whose main feature is a sellographic arm of a Basque pelota player. Produced with the Logo, elastic rubber bands, different balls, all items are fixed in different dimensions, creating movement and deconstruction of the window at the same time.

Client_ **LOREAK MENDIAN**   Design_ **JA! STUDIO**   Photography_ **FLORO AZQUETA**   Country_ **SPAIN**

Macy's Window Display

Macy's gave us the task to design its Holiday window display in their Miami Beach store. When we saw the space, we thought this was a great opportunity to experiment with typography. We decided to design the Macy's window display with these bases and using the words "give" and "believe" (Macy's promo word) we created the display using pins and over 3,000 yards of thread, the very material of fashion. We believe these materials and the way they were used allowed us to create an effect that emphasised and placed greater attention on the words and the holiday spirit.

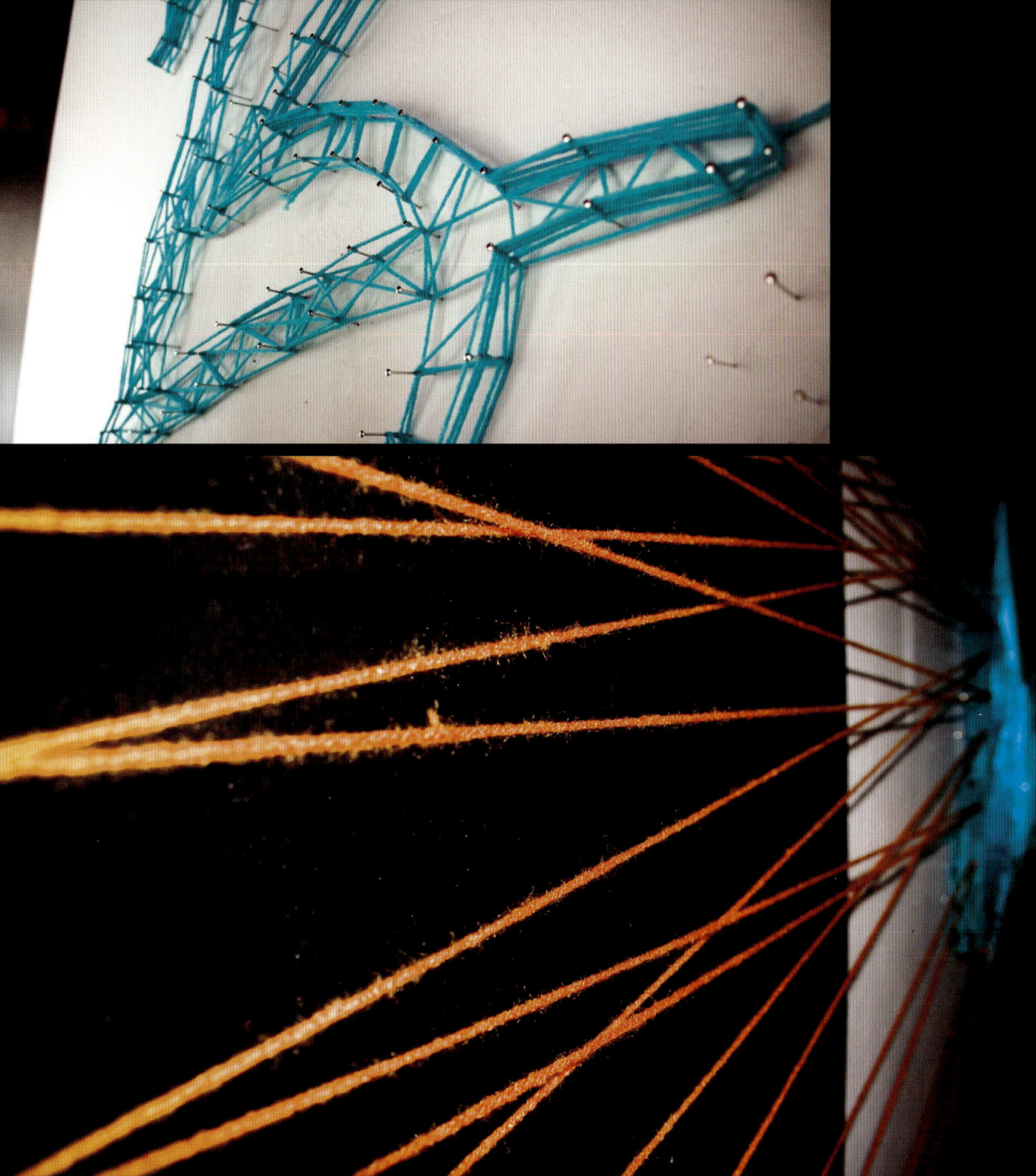

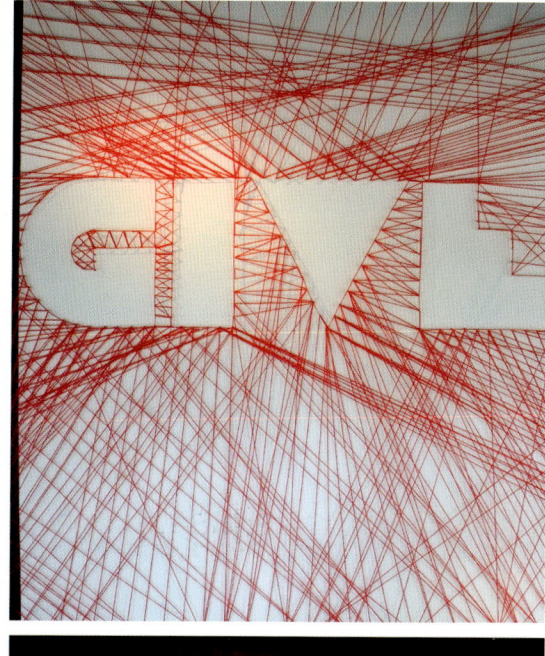

Client_ **MACY'S MIAMI**   Design team_ **DAVID GARCIA**   Photography_ **DAVID GARCIA**   Year of completion_ **2009**   Country_ **USA**
                                                    JUAN CAMILO ROJAS

RIBA REGENT STREET WINDOW PROJECT 2010

Hoss Intropia
Window Display

Client_ **HOSS INTROPIA**   Design_ **ELEANOR RENNIE**   Photography_ **MICHAEL LEWIS**   Year of completion_ **2010**   Country_ **UK**

RIBA REGENT STREET WINDOW PROJECT 2011

Duchamp Window Display

*T*his installation uses colours, shapes, objects, lights, and the images of onlookers, which are revealed and obscured. Each intake of the piece is different, each breath creates the world anew.
Through a variety of reflective surfaces an ever-changing pattern of movement is created, suggesting a breathing kaleidoscope that moves gradually in and out. Duchamp's richly patterned fabrics are framed and suspended between the movements and become part of the abstract dialogue with the street.
Passers-by, shoppers, moving buses and London's diverse streetscape are captured in fleeting moments, pulled in and pushed back in ever increasing and decreasing rhythms.

| Client_ **DUCHAMP** | Design_ **HONEY** | Photography_ **RALPH PARKER** | Year of completion_ **2011** | Country_ **UK** |

Banana Republic Window Display

U shida Findlay Architects and Visitor Studio collaborated to create a window installation for Banana Republic's Regent Street store. The client's brief was to create an eye catching piece, based around the themes of "Safari" and "Play".

It was our intention to create an installation that played with the relationship between the shop front glazing and the street. The final form appears as if a bucket of liquid had been splashed against the glass, with this moment captured and frozen in time. At the point were the splash hits the glass a larger silhouette of a safari scene is evident within the drips on the glass. The splash shape was generated with 3D digital sculpting techniques and then made into a plaster cast. A combination of eco-resin and laser cut plastic safari animals was poured into the cast to create the final splash form. The finished surface texture appears as if it is a mass of liquid melted plastic safari toys, in turn satisfying both aspects of the brief. The overall shape of the piece is intentionally directional carrying pedestrian's eye line from the splash's point of origin, the bucket, across the shape and into the shop. On some level this acts to direct foot fall into the retail space and attract peoples attention towards the interior and specifically the current fashion collection.

Client_ **BANANA REPUBLIC**   Design_ **USHIDA FINDLAY ARCHITECTS**   Photography_ **AGNESE SANVITO**   Year of completion_ **2012**   Country_ **UK**

Moss Bros Window Display

*D*elvendahl Martin Architects was selected by the RIBA (Royal Institute of British Architects) to create this temporary installation as part of the 2012 Regent Street Windows Project.

Working in collaboration with menswear brand Moss Bros as retailer partner, the idea was to make the most out of the windows of their shop located at the lower end of Regent Street in London. With a tangential take on the overall theme of "Play" as set by the program, the proposal sought to establish a playful relationship with the public by exaggerating the perspective and directing the attention towards specific areas of the display. This was achieved by stitching the edges of the window space to a series of frames at the centre using thousands of metres of waxed cotton string. The frames, which were perceived as seemingly floating voids, contained clothes representing the three different strands of the business. The installation was an exercise in the visual possibilities of the repetition of linear elements in terms of density and geometry, as well as colour and material to manipulate light. The material expression of the cotton strings recalled the raw materials of garments, the loom-based manufacturing process of cloth and the hand craftsmanship of the bespoke service that the company offers.

The project was approached and delivered in collaboration with a team of consultants that included the City University London's materials testing laboratory to establish the optimum thickness and strength for the cotton strings.

Client_ **MOSS BROS** | Design_ **DELVENDAHL MARTIN ARCHITECTS** | Photography_ **AGNESE SANVITO, GREG FONNE, NICK HOLT, HAYLEY MILLS** | Year of completion_ **2012** | Country_ **UK**

Ferrari Window Display

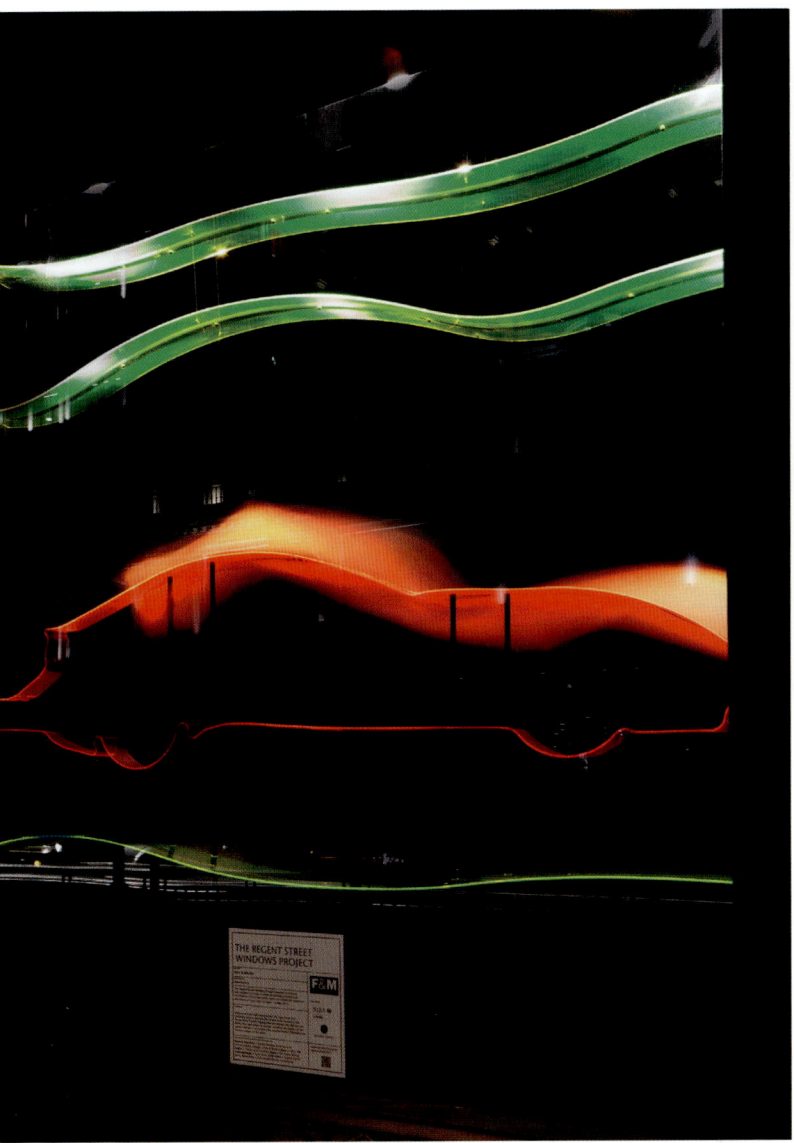

*W*ith the overarching theme "*Play*" we were keen to create an installation that introduces movement to the window display. Our proposal is inspired by the iconic shape of the Ferrari car and the way these shapes are tested in the wind tunnel.

Ribbons of neon light travel across the shop front space in a turbulent pattern, echoing the smoke trails created in the Ferrari wind tunnel. Fabric fixed to the back of the neon strips is blown about by wind machines and billows into different shapes. The ribbons at first glance seem chaotic but eventually take up the outline of the iconic Formula 1 car on one side, and the classic Gran Tourismo 4580 Ferrari car on the other.

Client_ **HABERDASHERY LONDON LTD.** | Design_ **FEIX&MERLIN ARCHITECTS** | Photography_ **SIMON MAXWELL AGNESE SANVITO** | Year of completion_ **2012** | Country_ **UK**

The Evolution Of Lightweight

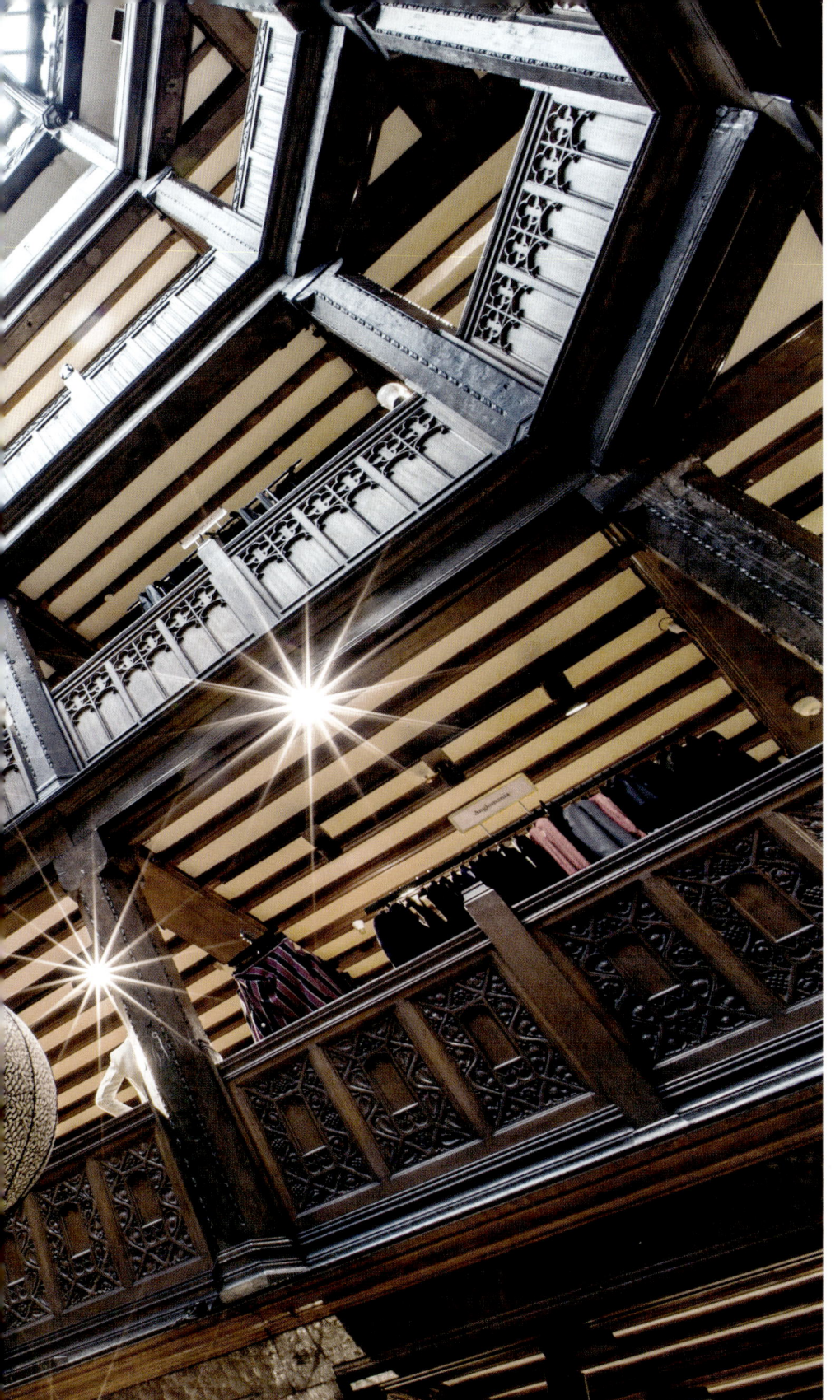

A *futuristic journey of Nike Running from pure*
performance to explosive style, which inspires
athletes to be the best they can be. This installation
focuses on the development of lightweight trainers and
apparel – the "Evolution Of Lightweight".

Skeleton In The Closet

This window started as a challenge to reuse garment shipment hangers in a unique way. Three days later, I found myself in my kitchen boiling hangers and molding them to a mannequin. The concept was to make a dress that would then grow up the side of the windows to complete the display. The frames were added to comment on the skeletal or frame like structure of the dress itself.

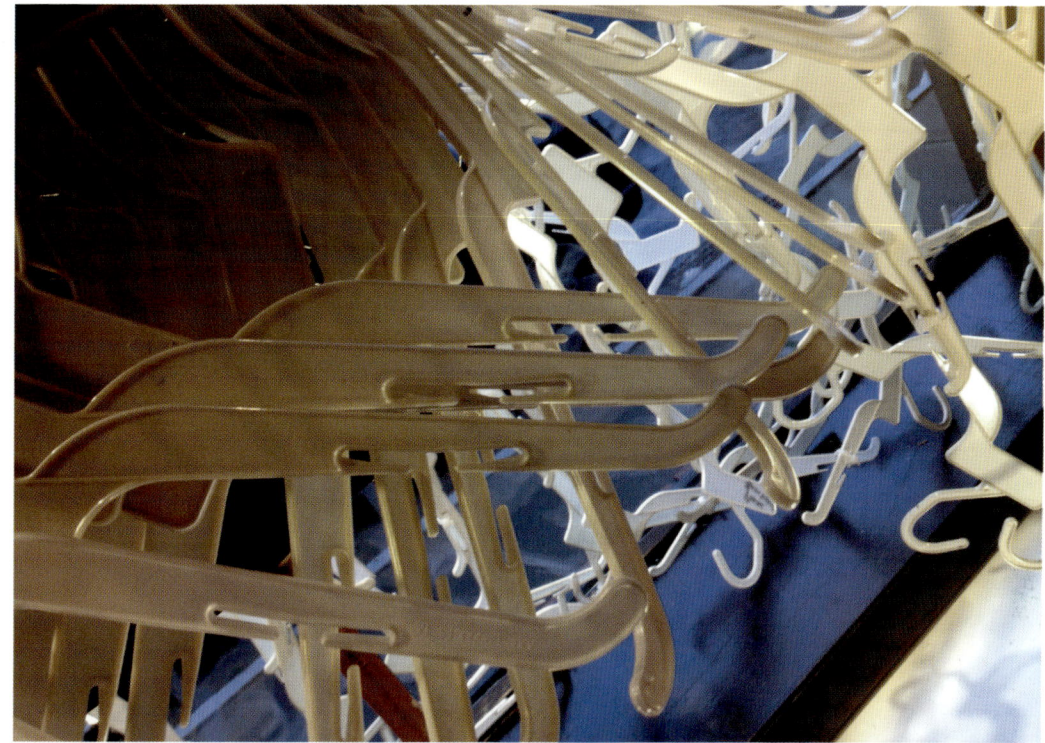

Client_ **SHOP PEPPERMINT**   Design_ **MELISSA MURPHY**   Photography_ **TANVI ASHER**   Year of completion_ **2012**   Country_ **USA**

SWAROVSKI
Window Display

*T*o surprise, to use the window display to create a brand: that is the goal. The 2012 Olympic Games in London, its international focus and the diversity of its visitors were the inspiration behind the portrayal of Swarovski's "Erica & Eliot around the world" characters and campaign. The various scenes take place on a map of the world in the window display version, or on a globe inside the store. As if through a magnifying glass and, with a notable reference to the world of comics, the transparent half-spheres show the characters and the branded product travelling around different parts of the world. In addition to the light, the rhythm and symmetry of the composition, the visual appeal is enhanced by the use of a very fresh colour scheme such as pink and green.

Noiselab – Cardboard Noise Window

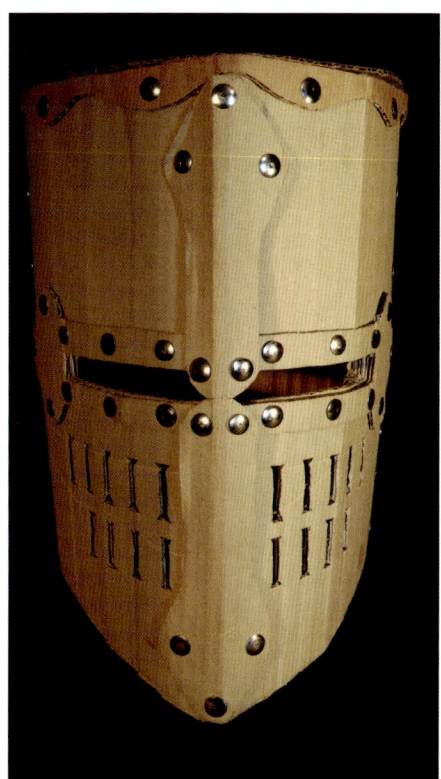

*N*oiseLab sold local artists' work, provided free advice, workshops and all sorts of amazing things to young artists local to Manchester. This window display was created to interest and entertain the public and to show off some of the fantastic t-shirts and artists' work for sale inside the shop.

As an artist, I use cardboard boxes in a seriously fun and creative way. The main idea for this project was to inject some of this fun, playful creativity into a shop window display and to promote an already very creative brand. The drum kit and guitar with amp were all created specially to fit with the theme of "Noise". Other items also added variety to the whole display.

Abington Window Display For Maven

*I*n an attempt to emulate Abington's aesthetics and authenticity of a well-bred working class, this display required recreating a scene found in rust belt communities. Cinder blocks, bricks, and metal found at the junkyard fashioned with dirt, vines, and leaves allowed the scene to have a post-industrial feel. Abington had additionally sent us images of northeastern autumn scenes and bricks with the logo etched into them. The images were set into frames and hung from the ceiling. Vinyl stickers designed to match the patterns within the lattice of the iron gate were applied to the outside of the building.

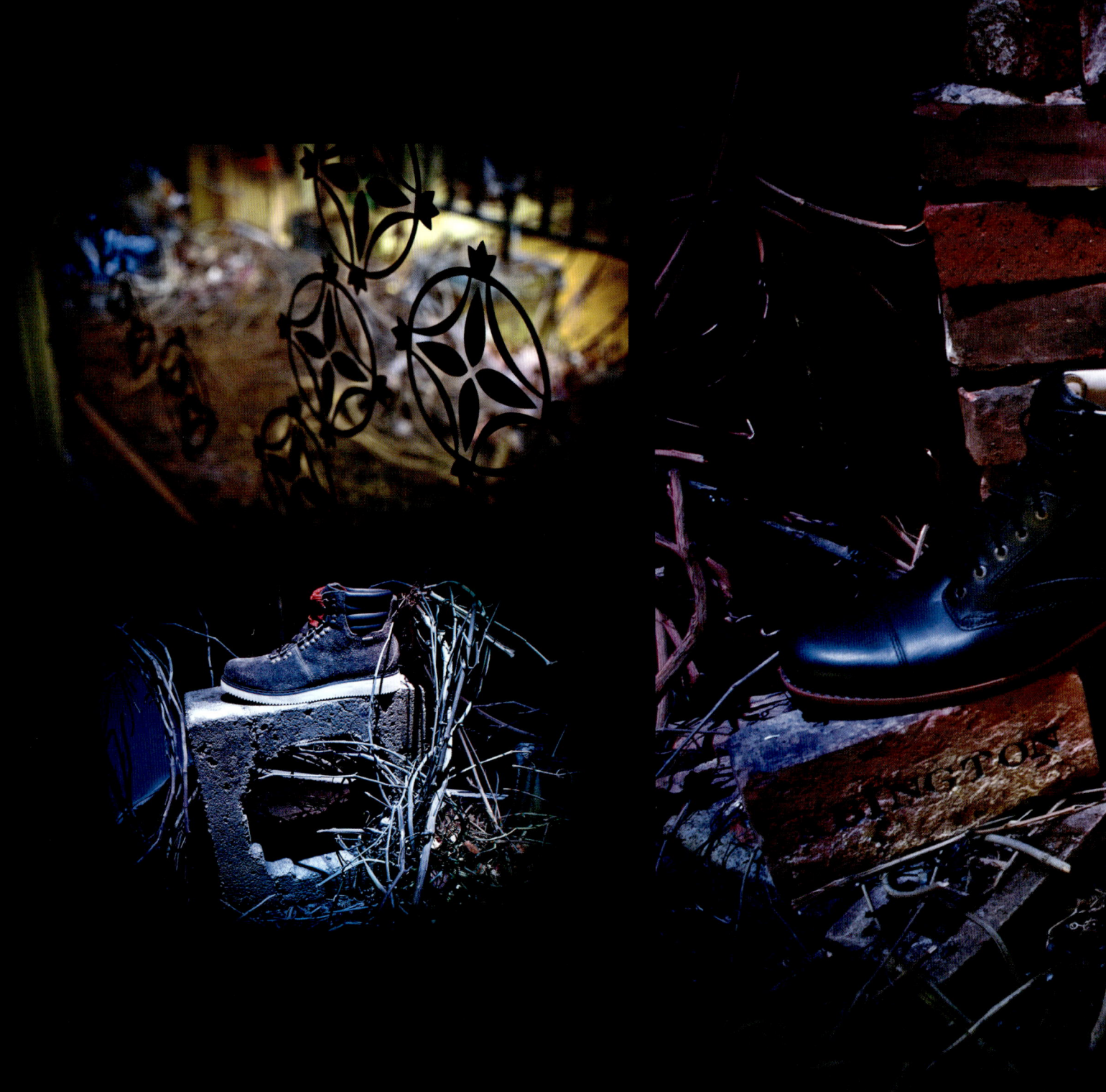

Client_ **MAVEN**   Design team_ **MICHAEL FAGAN**   Photography_ **MICHAEL FAGAN**   Year of completion_ **2010**   Country_ **USA**
BRENDAN FOSTER

Framed Up!

*T*his is the second time MISSONI and Havaianas collaborate. Like the collection, this window used earth-friendly materials. The whole window was covered by a zigzag pattern. Neon–painted wooden frames highlighted the Havaianas flip-flops at the center of each frame. A thin nylon thread was used to place the pairs inside the frame creating the illusion of floating flip-flops.

Client_ **HAVAIANAS PHILIPPINES** Design_ **JOJO ALVAREZ** Photography_ **JOJO ALVAREZ** Year of completion_ **2012** Country_ **PHILIPPINES**

Naked City Lampscapes

*N*aked City Lampscapes players on the relationship between two themes of the city and the mirror, resulting in a luminous skyline. This project started as a series of big lighting objects, realised in parchment paper. It was first presented at galleria Rossana Orlandi against the brilliant setting of the 2010 Milan Salone Del Mobile. Followed by this, designer Natascha Madeiski and architect Alexander Graef used cut out paper to create a wintry display for the two high-end fashion boutiques

Septieme Etage in Geneva.

The display utilises full scale moments and situations of their NAKED CITY range of paper lamps. It plays with urban scales and layers. Construction details are shown as shadows behind city façades, staircases in different directions can be discovered when looked at from certain angles. This playful idea of urban situations merged with construction details was realised in white Pergamenata paper in collaboration with Fedrigoni.

Client_ **SEPTIEME ETAGE BOUTIQUE**   Design team_ **ALEXANDER GRAEF NATASCHA MADEISKI**   Photography_ **ALEXANDER GRAEF NATASCHA MADEISKI**   Year of completion_ **2010**   Country_ **UK**

L'Oreal -
Maison Martin Margiela
Fragrance Window

L'Oreal appointed Elemental to design and produce in-store launch sites and a launch window at Selfridges, with an initial teaser campaign. Taking our reference from Margiela boutiques, exhibitions and books, Elemental Design set about expressing the brand's unique handwriting. Margiela use items such as old luggage, books and chairs, painted white, as part of their store merchandising. Margiela also use feathers (quill pens), wine bottles (table lamps) and many quirky, re-cycled objects to create their distinctive look. Elemental Design sourced dozens of items from car-boot sales, flea markets and second-hand stores, giving them the signature coat of white paint.

Madison Avenue [Doll] House

MADISON AVENUE [DOLL]HOUSE

design by REX ARCHITECTURE P.C.

structure by MAGNUSSON KLEMENCIC ASSOCIATES

fabrication by SITU STUDIO

REX is an internationally acclaimed architecture and design firm based in New York City. Buildings currently under construction include the Dallas Center for the Performing Arts Dee and Charles Wyly Theatre in Texas, Museum Plaza, a 62 - story art institute and mixed-use development in Louisville, Kentucky; and the Istanbul headquarters for Vakko, Turkey's preeminent fashion company. Founded in 2001 as OMA New York—the American branch of the Office for Metropolitan Architecture—REX became an independent office under the leadership of Joshua Prince - Ramus in 2006. At OMA New York, Mr. Prince - Ramus was Partner in Charge of the Seattle Central Library and the Guggenheim - Hermitage Museum in Las Vegas. REX recently participated in the limited competition to reconstruct Governors Island in New York Harbor, and is now engaged in the invited competition to design the new Edvard Munch Museum in Oslo, Norway. For more information, visit www.rexny.com

project team

óskar arnórsson, robert beach, jeff franklin, bassal gritt, sunnie joh, joshua prince ramus, jacob vidal, wes scoon, lavina sadhwani, alejandro schieda, ben strear, jay taylor, james white, eugenia zimmerman

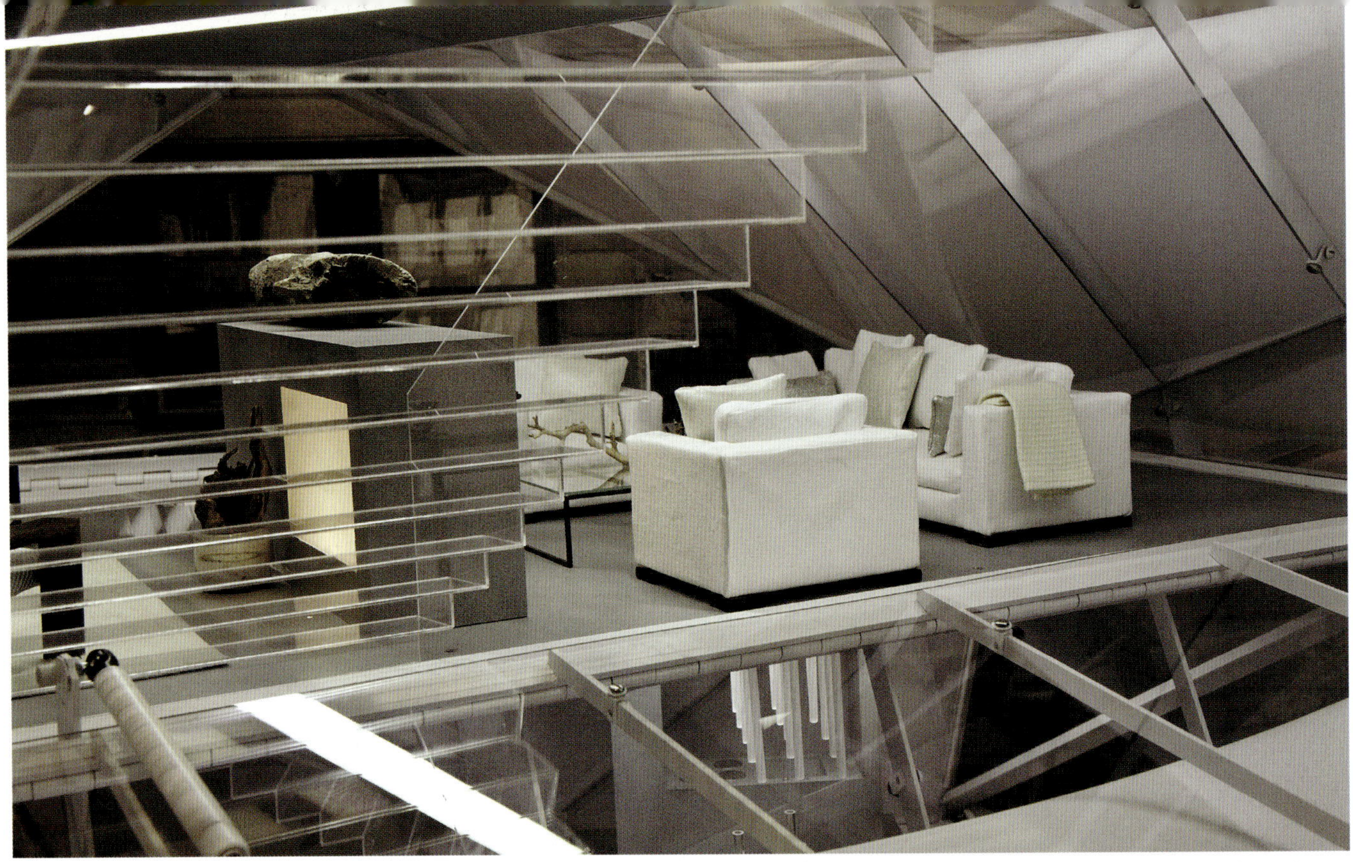

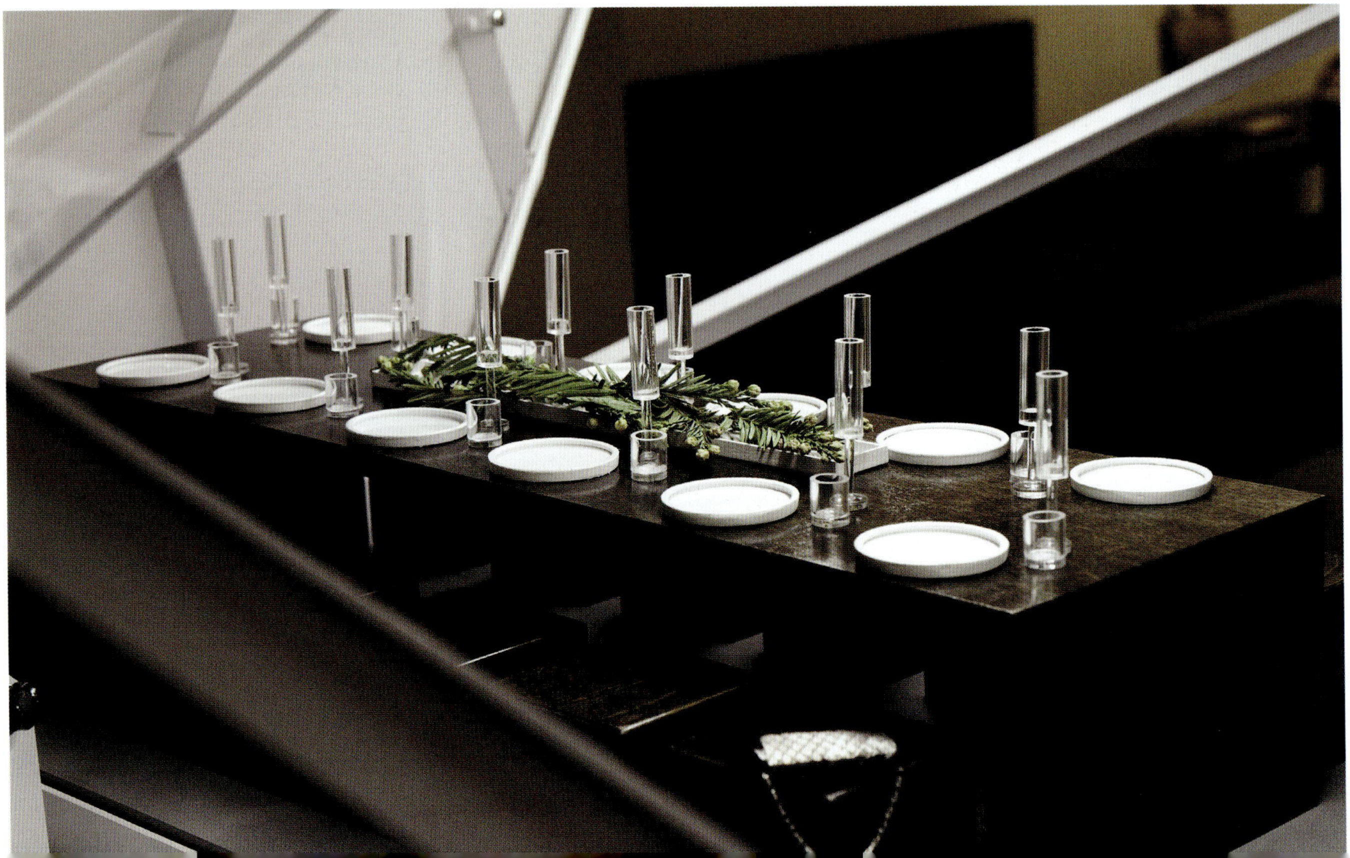

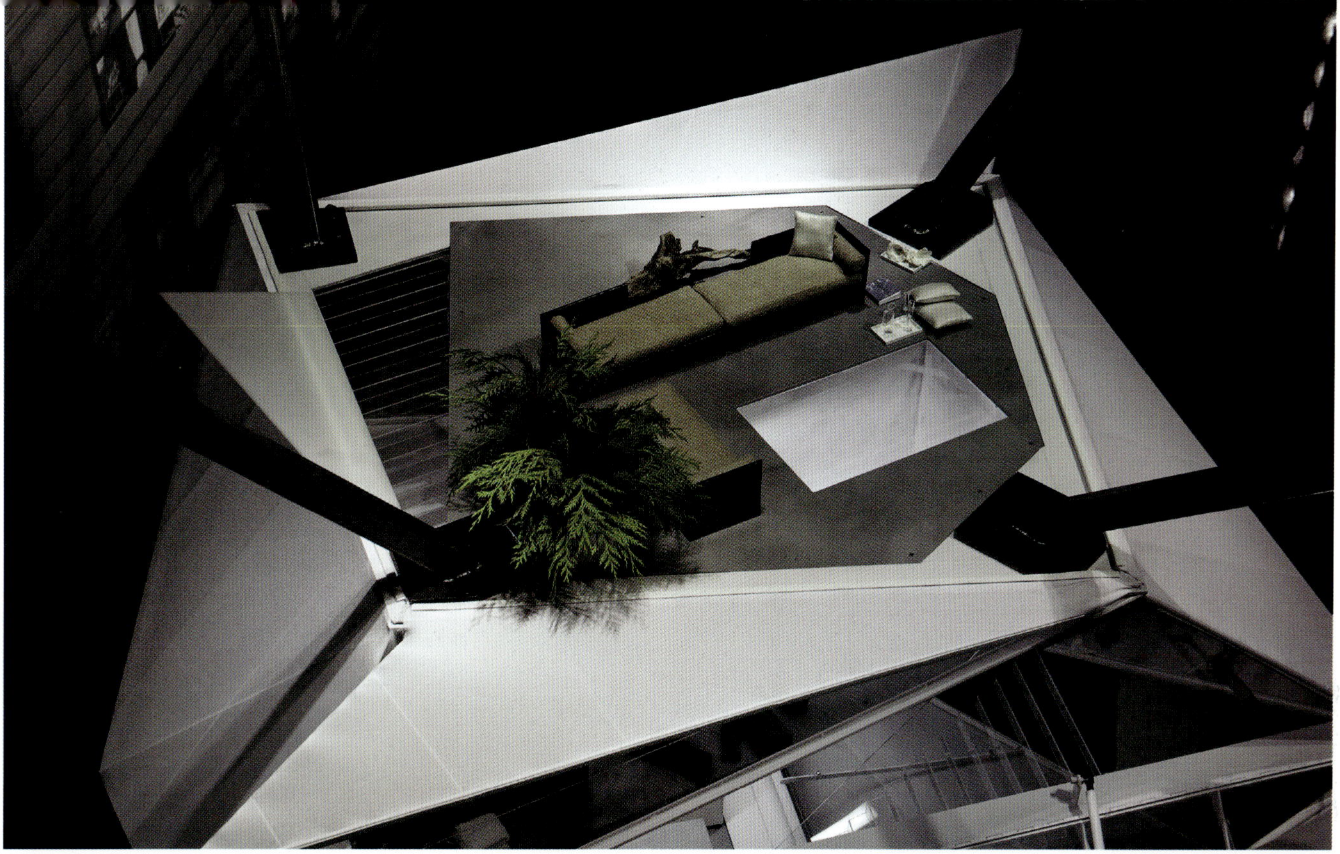

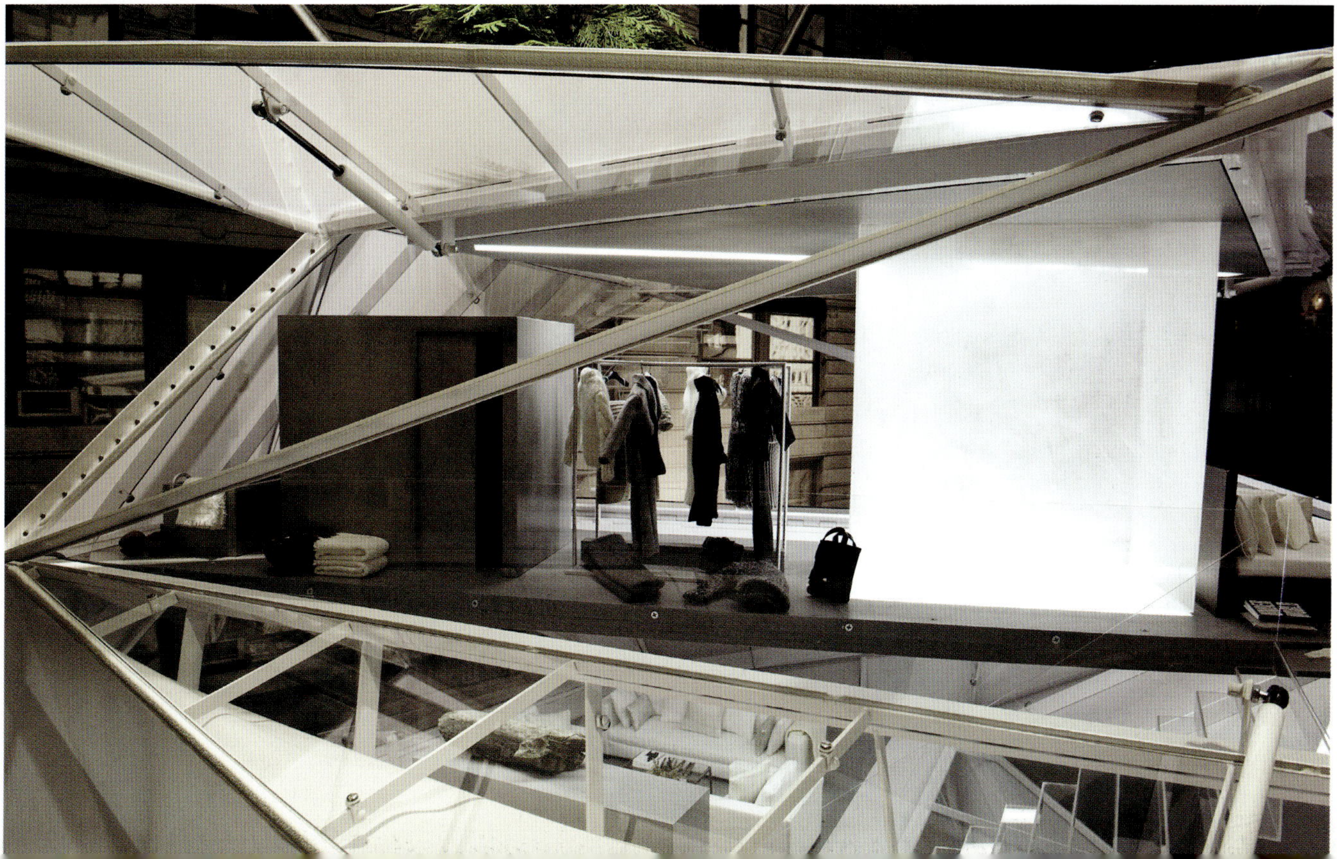

Calvin Klein's Senior Vice President for Creative Services approached REX to design a concept house showcasing pieces from the company's apparel, accessory, and home lines. The house would be realised in miniature and displayed in the main window of Calvin Klein's Madison Avenue store during the 2008-2009 holiday season. REX dubbed this fusion of concept house a "Doll House". For a practice committed to using constraints as generative opportunities, the project was challengingly whimsical, presenting an exciting and fun opportunity to test the limits of our methodology across multiple scales. A response to two markedly different scales and purposes, the Doll House had to reconcile — in one design — the contradictory constraints of a concept house and a doll house:

1. The concept house had to be designed for the "Calvin Klein Woman", a professed city-dweller; the doll house typology is traditionally a suburban, detached, single-family dwelling.

2. The concept house had to provide privacy for its hypothetical inhabitant; a doll house has to be open, at eye-level, and easily viewed in the round.

3. The concept house had to respect the minimalist aesthetic of Calvin Klein; the doll house had to be bold enough to attract the attention of holiday shoppers.

4. The concept house required a hypothetical site in New York City; the doll house site was already fixed — a Madison Avenue storefront. By siting the concept house in the "landscape" above a Manhattan intersection, the competing demands of the two scales begins to reconcile. Suspended in air, the concept house remains a freestanding residence while capitalising on underutilised urban space. Undeniably frivolous, the Madison Avenue [Doll]House nevertheless contains a kernel of an idea for accommodating growth in rapidly-densifying cities. Meanwhile, elevated and freestanding within the storefront, the doll house can be seen closely in the round and from afar, and can be opened from all sides for play.

The conflicting constraints that remained unresolved by the selection of the concept house's site are reconciled by the [Doll]House's design itself. The design begins as four, minimalist floor plates (dining room, living room, bedroom, and rooftop pool terrace) following the precedent set for Calvin Klein by John Pawson, the store's designer. The plates are then shifted to maximise visibility into the doll house, and to provide views out for the imagined occupant of the concept house. To balance the opposing desires for views and privacy, the [Doll]House is wrapped in a cocoon of translucent white textile. Conceptually, this fabric layer operates as a sunshade, outboard of a glass façade. The interiors and roof terrace are furnished with miniature replicas of pieces from the company's apparel, accessory, and home lines.

Client_ **CALVIN KLEIN, INC.**　Design_ **REX**　Photography_ **REX**　Year of completion_ **2008**　Country_ **USA**

Fabriano Boutique

W indow installations produced for Fabriano Boutique's spring 2011 collection and displayed in Milan, Rome, Florence and Munich. We created bold scenes of folded, layered and suspended birds carrying away a sculpted Fabriano bag. The unique backdrop is made up of interlocking birds that when closed, fold completely flat, but open out to become a striking three-dimensional flock.

The Last Winter

This project was designed for the autumn/winter window display for the UnCENSORED Store, inspired by the interpretation of different concepts of various fashion brands sold in this multi-store which are naturals, animals and graphic patterns. The deer's horn plays an important role as a winter symbol designed in geometric form together with the structures inspired by icebergs and printed backgrounds, depicting the mood of winter 2012: "The End is The New Beginning".

'END IS THE BEGINNING'

WINTER

Opening Ceremony
Pamela Love
Henrik Vibskov
Wood Wood
Saint Goya
Ganni
Minimarket
Happy Socks
Sundqvist
Surface To Air
MARCH LA.B
Trousers London
JS Lee London
Pijama
P.A.M.
E.L.K.E.
Venessa Arizaga
John Woo
Kawe:o

THE END IS THE
NEW BEGINNING'

Opening Cere
Pamela Love
Henrik Vibsk
Wood Wood
Lone Goya
Velour
Minimarket
Happy Socks
Sandqvist
Surface To Ai
MARCH LA.B
Trousers Lond
J&Lee London
Pijama
P.A.M.
E.L.K.E.
Venessa Ariza
John Woo
Kaweco

Message In A Bottle

*O*ver ten days, two families and one Teteria Gothic quarter helped us gather the material to create our "Message in a Bottle". The message would graph the amount of plastic we live with and convey the fact that recycling and / or reuse is not only an act of economic and ecological awareness, but also an exploration of different materials and a development of imagination and creativity to take them out of context.

It is a work that reuses plastic containers with a synthetic paint treatment forming a mountain inhabited by large wooden dolls with metal wigs.

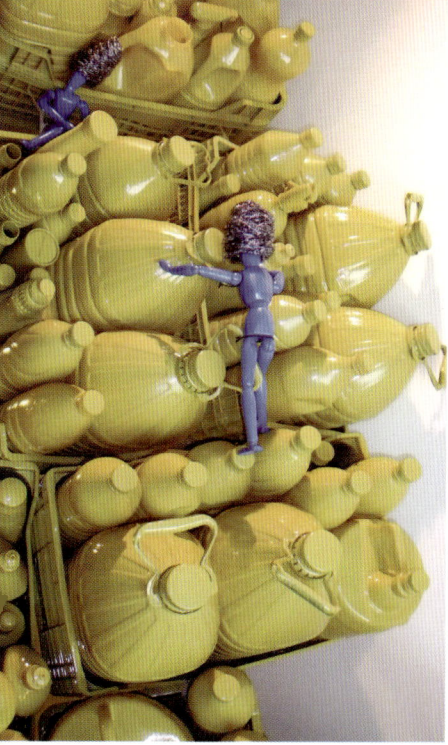

CONTEMPORARY
CHRISTMAS
ART

La Rinascente Vetrine Di Natale 2010

LAVA Christmas Windows Display

*L*aboratory for Visionary Architecture (LAVA) created a window installation for the famous Italian department store la Rinascente for its Vetrine di Natale 2010 [Christmas Windows].
LAVA's origami coral reef used 1500 recycled and recyclable cardboard molecules and explored the intelligence of natural and architectural systems. The sculpture played with space by climbing up walls and arching over to create coral caves. Based on the geometrical structures of sea foam and

corals, the colourful reef came to life through dynamic lighting and sound. Chris Bosse, director of multinational LAVA, was one of seven designers from around the world to be commissioned to create a window for this brand. The store windows were at la Rinascente at Piazza Duomo, in the centre of Milan, design capital of the world. This was the first time la Rinascente commissioned artists to do Christmas windows. The installation showed how a particular module, copied from nature, can

generate architectural space, and how the intelligence of the smallest unit dictates the intelligence of the overall system. Ecosystems such as coral reefs act as a metaphor for an architecture where the individual components interact in symbiosis to create an environment.
Bosse says: "In urban terms, the smallest homes, the spaces they create, the energy they use, the heat and moisture they absorb, multiply into a bigger organisational system, whose sustainabilty depends on their intelligence".
Current trends in parametric modeling, digital fabrication and material-science were applied to the space-filling installation.

Client_ **LA RINASCENTE**   Design_ **LAVA - LABORATORY FOR VISIONARY ARCHITECTURE**   Photography_ **FILIPPO PATRESE**   Year of completion_ **2010**   Country_ **ITALY**

CONTEMPORARY
CHRISTMAS
ART

LA RINASCENTE VETRINE DI NATALE 2011

Clockwork Snow

*M*echanical gears seem to drop from heaven like icy snowflakes, crystallising into a magical machine frozen in time. The gears represent our rational world, but here they transcend the purely utilitarian to become a romantic, haunting dream.

Tjep. was invited amongst six other international artists and designers to create a Christmas window for Italy's most famous department store La Rinascente on Piazza Duomo in Milano.

Client_ **LA RINASCENTE**   Design_ **TJEP.**   Design team_ **FRANK TJEPKEMA LEONIE JANSSEN**   Photography_ **TJEP.**   Year of completion_ **2011**   Country_ **ITALTY**

Eternal Spring

W hen planning the window of "Eternal Spring" for
*nunoya, we wanted to reflect the first impression
when people think of Japanese nature. It had to be a tree,
lit by the rising sun.*
*We created curved branches, which transmit fluency and
express the oriental spirit. The characteristic shapes of the
trees, combined with the fabric of the house, have helped
us to achieve a display that delights the eye of interns and
customers, and promotes the good work of its owners and
employees.*

Client_ **STORE NUNOYA BARCELONA** | Design_ **VENTANUZKA STUDIO** | Photography_ **VALERIA MORGANTI** | Year of completion_ **2010** | Country_ **ARGENTINA**

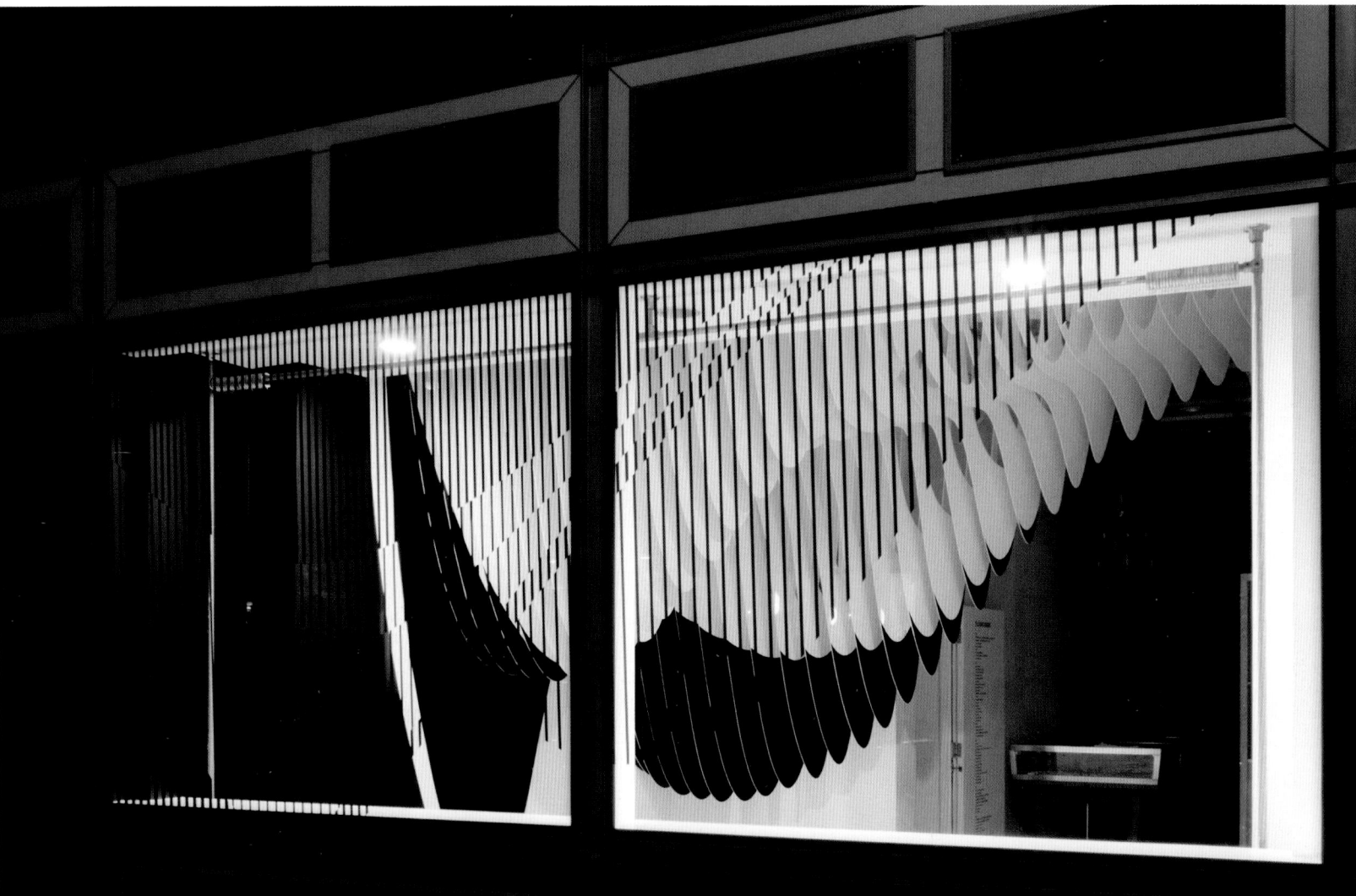

Aqua
At Dover Street Market

*D*over Street Market commissioned Zaha Hadid to design a site-specific installation to be showcased in their London store during the 2012 Olympic Games. Entitled "Aqua", the concept references the formal language of Hadid's renowned London Aquatics Centre. "Designing for Dover Street Market is an exciting opportunity to install a piece inspired by the fluid geometries of the London Aquatics Centre: a wave of liquid, frozen in time, right in the heart of London", said Hadid.

The installation will be on display at Dover Street Market for the duration of the Olympic and Paralympic Games.

Design_ **ZAHA HADID ARCHITECTS**   Photography_ **JAMES HARRIS**   Year of completion_ **2012**   Country_ **UK**

Paper Prada

*T*his is a new Prada campaign showcasing looks from Prada's
   Spring/Summer 2012 collection as well as illustrated props
created by Coco Brun alongside Anna Sbiera and Delphine Roche.
"Paper Prada" was photographed by Marc da Cunha Lopes and
features two striking young models showing off a collection of high
end swimwear and evening looks.

Asmaul Husna

*E*id is one of the biggest national holidays in Indonesia. The concept of the holy holiday is the return to "Fitri". We tried to present a simple yet religious window display theme for the store, Asmaul Husna, which means "the names of Allah", consists of the 99 natures of Allah. White resembles the pureness of the whole event and the tree on which the names were hung depicts how comfortable life is under the auspices of the greatness of Allah.

MAAN
ADA
A BINTANG
HON YANG
AN TIDAK
N TIDAK
ETUNJUK
A. ALLAH
AN ALLAH

YANG MAHA PEMURAH. YANG MAHA PENGASIH.
MAHA RAJA, MAHA SUCI. MAHA SEJAHTERA. YANG
MAHA TERPERCAYA. YANG MAHA MEMELIHARA.
YANG MAHA PERKASA. YANG MEMBUAT BENTUK.
YANG MAHA PENGAMPUN. YANG MAHA PERKASA.
YANG PEMBERI YANG MAHA PEMBERI REZKI.
YANG MAHA PEMBUKA HATI. YANG MAHA
MENGETAHUI. YANG MAHA PENGENDALI YANG
MAHA MELAPANGKAN. YANG MERENDAHKAN.
YANG MENINGGIKAN. YANG MAHA TERHORMAT.
YANG KEHENDAKNYA TIDAK DAPAT DIINGKARI.
YANG MEMILIKI KEBESARAN. YANG MAH.
PENCIPTA. YANG MENGADAKAN DARI TIADA. YANG
MAHA MENGHINAKAN. YANG MAHA MENDENGAR.
YANG MAHA MELIHAT. YANG MEMUTUSKAN
HUKUM. YANG MAHA ADIL. YANG MAHA LEMBUT.
YANG MAHA MENGETAHUI. YANG MAHA
PENYANTUN. YANG MAHA PENYANTUN. YANG
MAHA AGUNG. YANG MAHA PENGAMPUN. YANG
MENERIMA SYUKUR. YANG MAHA TINGGI. YANG

ASMAUL HUSN
"MILIK ALLAH-LAH NAMA-NAMA YA
INDAH, DAN BERMOHONLAH
KEPADA-NYA DENGAN MENYEBUT
NAMA-NAMA TERSEBUT"

Client_ **ALUNALUN INDONESIA KREASI**   Design team_ **ARDAN HANAFI, MERDEKA AGNIKARMA, ALVINDRA ADHIKRESNA, ZANUN NURANGGA**   Year of completion_ **2007**   Country_ **INDONESIA**

Il Gufo

*I*l Gufo is a leading Italian luxury clothing brand for children, specialised in designing, producing and distributing unique, high quality collections for children from 0 to 14.

Window projects by Francesca Signori has the same language: quality of the materials, attention to details, exclusivity of manufacturing.

Replay Barcelona

*R*eplay's store on Passeig de Gràcia in Barcelona now hosts a vertical garden of just above 100m². In the storefront location, the two storey wall is set in a dramatic and playful environment designed by Studio 10, with waterfalls, sculptures and contrasting materials. As a great place to study nature's own vertical gardens, the waterfalls were a natural starting point for the plant design. Looking closer to the environment around a waterfall, growing conditions change with linear patterns of fissures and cracks in the underlying exposed rock, or the rapidly decreasing moisture already small steps away from the immediate vicinity of the falling water. In such a manner, like the erratic and geometric cracking of an eroding rock, groups and strings of plants were laid out in an organic pattern. The generous surface allow for many kinds of plants. Larger groups of begonias, different ferns, small but long aroids like the common *Philodendron scandens* or *Scindapsus pictus*, sets the background for more dramatic effects of cascading fronds of *Nephrolepis exaltata* and *Polypodium subauriculatum* or larger aroids like *Philodendron giganteum* and *P. erubescens.* >>

The store also has an outdoor vertical garden, located in a patio in the back of the store. Partially shadowed by surrounding buildings, the southwest facing wall has the upper area well exposed to the hot Mediterranean sun, whereas the lower part is mostly in shadow. This difference in sun exposure gave way for more typical Mediterranean plants in the top – such as Lavandula, Rosmarinus and Artemisia – and more shadow preferring plants like Chlorophytum and Fatsia in the lower area. In between there are a few plants that will gain some size, the idea being to create a strong and wild growing surface, contrasting the metal grid from which it extends.

Get Into Spring

*T*OMS in the UK gave me the amazing opportunity to design a unique window project for the spring season. TOMS wanted to spread awareness of their "One for One" movement when a child in need is given a pair of shoes for every pair that is bought. This window was successful in helping sell hundreds of shoes within days of installing it.

Client_ **TOMS SHOES**   Design_ **GAVIN DIAS**   Art direction_ **ALEXANDER STOAKES**   Photography_ **LOVEMEKNOTTS**   Year of completion_ **2012**   Country_ **UK**

RIBA REGENT STREET WINDOW PROJECT 2010

Oasis Window Display

*T*he installation was designed by award-winning architects Hawkins\Brown in collaboration with internationally renowned artist Bob and Roberta Smith and apiarist James Hamill.

Unveiled during the London Festival of Architecture 2010, a citywide festival celebrating London's urban past, present and future, the installation was programmed as part of the Regent Street Windows initiative. The installation drew inspiration from the book A World Without Bees:

"Honeybees are disappearing at an alarming rate. In America, one in three hives was left lifeless at the beginning of 2008. One third of what we eat, and much of what we wear, relies on pollination by honeybees." Bees play a vital role in the fashion industry in pollinating plants used for fabric. Their decline in numbers in the last 20 years poses a threat to the fashion industry, which currently contributes £200m per annum to the UK economy. The humble bee provides the perfect metaphor for civic and social harmony; representing feudal hierarchy, absolute monarchy, republicanism, capitalist industry, and commerce as well as socialist aspirations; the hive being a place of co-operative and collaborative working and living much like our cities and towns. Living in London, we often speak of making our own urban oasis, a place to escape to. The Oasis installation cultivated fragrant lavender to create an oasis for the humble bee and in doing so created a slice of paradise for passers-by to escape the hubbub and pollution of the city. At the centre of the installation nestled a cluster of working hives lent by the apiarist James Hamill which was a bespoke 21st Century "hive" created especially for the window. The "Cor-bee Cube" is a miniature replica of the new arts and civic building designed by Hawkins\Brown in the East Midlands town of Corby. Bob and Roberta Smith's Hollywood sign sculpture "Grow Lavender" gently illuminated the fragrant shrubs surrounding it with its strong call to action.

'Oasis in the city'

Oasis teams up with architects Hawkins\Brown, artist Bob and Roberta Smith and beekeeper James Hamill to create a truly beautiful 'Oasis' in the city.

LONDON FESTIVAL OF ARCHITECTURE
19 JUNE – 4 JULY 2010
WWW.LFA2010.ORG

204

Electro Garden

*I*t should be noted that in some studies, we like to leave a bit of improvisation during assembly. That day, we loaded Tomato "junk" left on the ground a mountain of thousands of useless appliances painted green. The truth is that the life of the windows is temporary and fleeting. However, the flowered green waterfall is a concept that implies that nature triumphs nonetheless.

Client_ **TOMATE STORE BARCELONA** | Design_ **VENTANUZKA STUDIO** | Photography_ **MARA PODOROISKY** | Year of completion_ **2009** | Country_ **ARGENTINA**

Replay Florence

*T*he project at the new Replay concept store in Florence was completed in spring 2009, at the time of the opening. The Italian architectural firm STUDIO10 based in Florence has chosen Vertical Garden Design for the installation of this green artwork. The vertical garden was inscribed in the experimental environment of the new retail concept designed by the architectural firm for Replay and tested for the first time in Florence. The green installation covers a 7m high L-shaped wall in the three-storey boutique. The garden is inspired by the undergrowth of a temperate forest, similar to what could be found in the lower parts of the hills not too far away from the city of Florence. Although as with any indoor garden, the plants themselves has to be mostly of tropical origin to do well in the indoor climate. The overall picture is a soft, yet dense, and fresh greenery, with some small-flowering plants like lanterns on top of the darker background. It is a picture that's reminiscent of the undergrowth in springtime, when it has had time to grow before the leaves of the canopy have fully developed and absorbed all incoming light.

There is a base of plants with medium sized leaves, like Aglaonema, Philodendron, Syngonium, Microsorum and a few other ferns as well. Within this framework, there are solitary species with stronger characters – like Begonia, Asparagus and Peperomia - some that are flowering, others with special coloured or textured leaves. Usually, not too many solitary species are necessary to give the garden a distinct character, and actually a sparse use of these plants may better bring out their unique qualities.

As the wall is used as background for displaying the brand's jeans products, hanging close to the wall, there is a limited space for using more voluminous plants. Thus, the size and growth habit were important criteria when choosing the plants. But still, as with any of these gardens, a certain pruning is necessary to keep a long-term viable garden.

Client_ **REPLAY**　　　　Design_ **VERTICAL GARDEN DESIGN**　　　　Year of completion_ **2009**　　　　Country_ **ITALY**

Chopard Animal World
At Selfridges

*F*or their 150th anniversary, Chopard created 14 limited-edition watches, each with an endangered animal species on its face. To be launched in Selfridges' Wonder Room, Rachael Bingham from Chopard briefed Elemental Design to create bespoke settings depicting the natural habitats of the creatures around all enchanting pop-up book. Elemental Design made these in a pale palette, from a combination of papers, frosted acrylics and flocked acrylics. Paper sculptor, Andrew MacGregor, crafted an origami animal for each scene. To create a narrative, Gary Porter wrote charming "grown-up" fairytales about each animal.

In the snowy mountains of ancient Bhutan, it is said that only one precious panda warrior remains, a female called Pandora. She lives in the foothills, in a dense bamboo forest. They say she is 150 years old. Some suspect Pandora has had more than a little 'work' done, although it's not true. Many have died trying to reach her to learn her secrets. They undertake the hazardous journey from city to mountain top because it is said that when you gaze into those wise, black, jewel-like eyes, you will grasp Pandora's key to eternal youth.

Chopard

ANIMAL WORLD
by
Chopard

Topshop Caravan Window

*T*opshop's creative team came up with a Summer Festival concept, featuring a life-size caravan, parked in a field. Elemental Design built the retro-style caravan, sliced at a cross-section to expose its interior, for Topshop's Oxford Street flagship.

It was tailor-made from scratch, in Elemental Design's workshops, rather than salvaging a real "recreational vehicle" - in order to make transporting and installation more practical. The caravan was parked in a summery meadow-scene which Elemental Design's team meticulously recreated.

Client_ **TOPSHOP**   Design_ **ELEMENTAL DESIGN LTD**   Photography_ **KATE WESTGATE**   Year of completion_ **2009**   Country_ **UK**

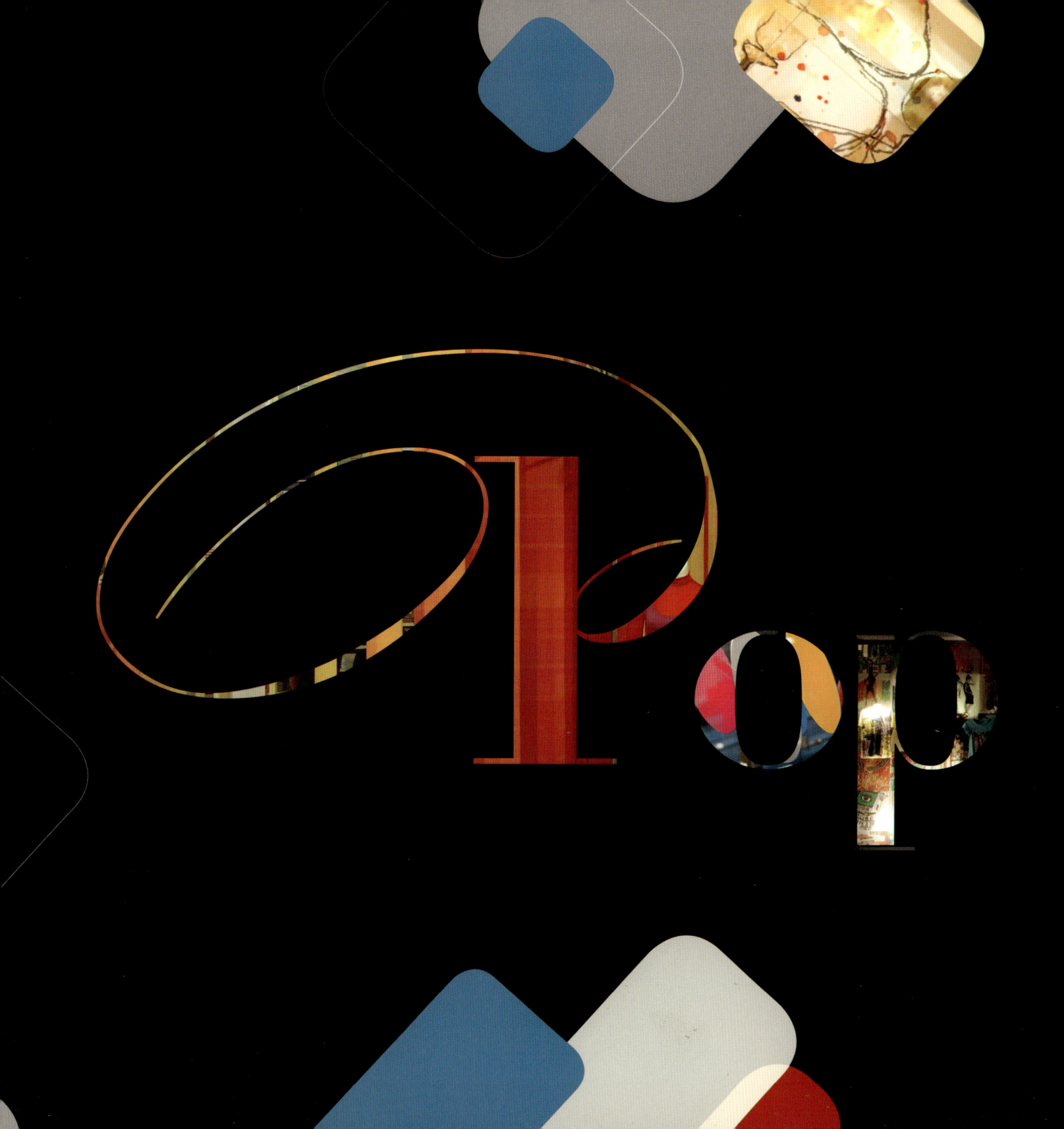

RIBA PLAY YOUR STYLE @ XINTIANDI, SHANGHAI 2012

Dexter Moren Associates ✕ Franc Franc

Collaborating with Japanese retailer Francfranc, Dexter Moren Associates have designed a window display based on the game "Mikado", where coloured sticks are dropped and players have to skilfully remove their chosen colours. DMA created a super scale version of the game using bamboo scaffolding to form self-supporting structures on the façade of the shop that are internally lit at night.

Client_ **FRANC FRANC**   Design_ **DEXTER MOREN ASSOCIATES**   Photography_ **JAN SIEFKE**   Year of completion_ **2012**   Country_ **UK**

Riba Paly Your Style @ Xintiandi, Shanghai 2012
All Design × SMUDGE

All Design's proposal for Smudge blurs the boundaries between art, architecture and retail. Camouflage patterns engulf the mannequins and the window, while fans positioned within circulate hundreds of small bullets and balloons around the void. The display responds to the brand's motto: "Still Moving UnDer GunfirE".

Client_ **SMUDGE**   Design_ **ALL DESIGN**   Photography_ **JAN SIEFKE**   Year of completion_ **2012**   Country_ **UK**

Uniqlo Heattech Project 2010 : Branded Art Installation

" *Aurora Borealis* " *was a branded art installation which had been commissioned as part of Uniqlo's Heattech campaign for their flagship store in New York. The goal was to make a high-impact installation that evokes HEAT and TECH – the two key selling points of this product line. The creative response deliberately chose "no-tech " to express "high-tech " in order to create an immersive and poetic intervention in the space through simple sculptural forms that emit a luminescent aura without relying on expensive lighting technology. With*

the ultimate goal to effectively communicate and transmit the feeling of being immersed in "heat", a series of two to four-metre tall "fins", with gradated colour fields, were composed precisely throughout the space to create a singular monolithic fractal icon that changed and transformed according to the viewer's point of view – a non-static static form. The combined visual results kinetic energy captured in a frozen moment, a sense of light without light, a powerful visual magnet in the midst of the busiest retail street of New York Soho.

Client _ **UNIQLO** | Design _ **MONA KIM: PROJECTS** | Design team _ **NEW PROJECT LLC LET THERE BE NEONS** | Photography _ **MONA KIM: PROJECTS** | Year of completion _ **2010** | Country _ **FRANCE**

Uniqlo
XXL Space Invader
Origami Santas

For Uniqlo's holiday environment, the creative challenge was to find a new approach to express this season — the time of the year with such high commercial pressure — without compromising the edgy techno-human soul of the brand.

How can familiar symbols be rendered in a fresh and contemporary manner? A slightly dark sense of humor seemed to be the answer: Taking a banal icon-Santa-and giving him a twist...a bit "kowaii" (scary) and a bit "kawaii" (cute) at the same time. The end result was a bizarre hybrid between a Santa and a Space Invader. Referencing these qualities so characteristic of Japanese mangas was one way to bring in the pop

factor to the good (but over-used) Santa and staying true to the "no-nonsense / rigorous / quirky / humanoid / off" spirit of the brand's visual approach. The process involved researching origami forms that exist in the world, then making concerted choices that would be most brand-appropriate. The exciting and challenging part of the project was the R&D phase to find ways to adapt the forms to be buildable at a super-scale of 3 - 4 meters (10 - 13 ft.) in a seamless manner, which would impact the space in a powerful manner.

Uniqlo Cargo & Chino Campaign 2011

We installed a 3D window display for Uniqlo's Spring Cargo & Chino campaign. Alongside the usual vinyl and printed graphics, we created a series of giant 3D tags which can be seen here hanging in the windows of their flagship stores in Oxford Street.

Client_ **UNIQLO**   Design_ **BRANCH**   Design team_ **TIJL SCHNEIDER PAUL FOX SARAH PARKER**   Photography_ **PAUL FOX**   Year of completion_ **2011**   Country_ **UK**

Uniqlo UT 2011

Uniqlo's world famous T-shirts are brought to life using a diverse range of imagery. We designed and produced graphics and supporting materials for every store in the UK.

KOKAKU KIDOTAI

"Kokaku Kidotai" is the definitive animated series of the eponymous sci-fi comic franchise. In the year 2030, society is on a one-way street to chaos as information networks develop at break-neck speed empowering criminals in new and dangerous ways. In the midst of this turmoil, there is one group brave enough to search out the causes of these crimes and put a stop to them before they start. The series follows the adventures of the Department of Internal Affairs' Public Safety Section Number 9, commonly referred to as Kokaku Kidotai.

Client_ **UNIQLO** Design_ **BRANCH** Design team_ **TIJL SCHNEIDER PAUL FOX** Photography_ **PAUL FOX** Year of completion_ 2012 Country_ **UK**

Uniqlo Spring Campaign 2012

We were asked to inject some colour and impact into all the Uniqlo stores. Using the pastel colour palette of the current collection, we produced bespoke perspex circles and designed vinyls to compliment them graphically.

We rolled the campaign across all Uniqlo's major London stores including their new store in Stratford Westfield.

Client_ **UNIQLO**   Design_ **BRANCH**   Design team_ **TIJL SCHNEIDER PAUL FOX**   Photography_ **PAUL FOX**   Year of completion_ **2012**   Country_ **UK**

Original Penguin Window Display

*M*y window display shows the outside (left window) and the inside (right) of the secret speakeasy culture. The left window shows a penguin manning the hatch, making sure the place stays secret from other birds, such as a flamingo. The right shows a vast number of penguins enjoying themselves with taboo luxuries. A possible idea to go along with this display is to have real live penguins in the shop window as a stunt to increase the buzz and popularity within the brand.

Custo Barcelona

*T*he designer Francesca Signori interpreted the
Custo Barcelona line with colours, light, flowers
and crystals for all US stores

Client_ **CUSTO BARCELONA US STORE**   Design_ **FRANCESCA SIGNORI**   Photography_ **FRANCESCA SIGNORI**   Year of completion_ **2012**   Country_ **US**

10

A window display marking the 10th anniversary of the San Sebastián flagship store, featuring a waterproof jacket from the autumn/winter collection supported by a structure of four folding chairs.

Institutional Sinfonia

*T*he idea was to consolidate the brand's two stores with a single image. We proposed something simple, with personality: The whole window has a touch of melody, arising out of a set of items, while the summer breeze seeps through an open door. Biu was a shop-studio where creations were made each season, from the choice of colour, design and fabrics. So this time we chose to reuse the cardboard tubes used to wind fabrics and transform them into a musical instrument of inspiration for the new season.

Window Display For A Shoe Shop

S *et of illustrations for a window display in a*
Bordeaux shoe shop.

It's A Fantasy

*H*ow lowly flip-flops are considered high-fashion is indeed a fantasy. This window showcases the collaboration of MISSONI and Havaianas for 2011. With elements of surrealism, this window display highlights the MISSONI patterns printed on the soles of the flip-flops. The black flip-flops, which were meant to mimic the grass, black sand and black diamond-shaped pedestals create that exact surreal mood.

Odel Window Display

Redefining everything we ever thought about window shopping! As a mix of art, fashion, design and marketing, we not only try to grab attention but also compel customers to enter our store. With distinctive conceptualizing, planning and installing, the creative windows define our brand's image.

FREE SHIPPING
FREE SHIPPING
FREE SHIPPING
ENGLAND
CHAMPION OF LIBERTY
STATES POSTAGE

Adidas Skateboarding Window Display For Maven

With no budget and little to work with, we used things from around the shop to create the window display. Hand-made frames were cut from a plank in the basement and then stained to look nice. Signatures from the Adidas skateboarding team riders were cut into vinyl decals and placed on wood pedestals to feature the pro model sneakers. Additional decals of the Adidas logos were cut to be placed on the window. Lightbulbs were hung from the ceiling, a mat was placed on the floor, and a plant sits in the window, giving a nice, simple aesthetic.

Client_ **MAVEN**   Design team_ **MICHAEL FAGAN BRENDAN FOSTER**   Photography_ **MICHAEL FAGAN**   Year of completion_ **2011**   Country_ **USA**

UnCENSORED
Window Display

Venessa Arizaga
John Woo
Kaweco

This window display was designed for Spring Summer UnCENSORED muti-brand store in Bangkok. The sculptural form inspired by geometric form related to the clothes collection's prints and patterns and added a glimpse of spring summer by using wood.

Client_ **UNCENSORED** | Design_ **THANWIN KAMYEAM** | Photography_ **THANWIN KAMYEAM** | Year of completion_ **2012** | Country_ **THAILAND**

Port To Port

*W*e left the port of Barcelona and after several trips landed in Buenos Aires. The first thing we saw was the natural light coming through huge windows, and this was our starting point of inspiration. The idea was to enhance the warmth of the light, reuse, filter, make play with inside the room, and get the effect caused by the sun of the day and remain at sunset. Fabrics were reused to make racks in reflectors.

Client_ **MOEBIUS STORE SAN TELMO**   Design_ **VENTANUZKA STUDIO**   Photography_ **MARA PODOROISKY**   Year of completion_ **2012**   Country_ **ARGENTINA**

Summer Of Sight

I was again offered the chance to produce some window imagery for TOMS summer eyewear campaign. For every pair of sunglasses bought, they gave someone their sight back via surgery, glasses or medical treatment and they successfully did this for 100,000 people! The window also helped sell many units of TOMS sunglasses.

Client_ **TOMS SHOES**   Design_ **GAVIN DIAS**   Design team_ **ALEXANDER STOAKES,**   Photography_ **JEREMY HOSKING**   Year of completion_ **2012**   Country_ **UK**

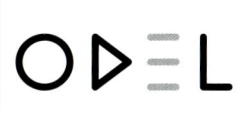

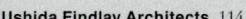